ANIMA ASTROLOGIAE

originally published as
Anima Astrologiae, or A Guide For Astrologers
Being The Considerations of the famous Guido Bonatus

Compiled in 1675 by
William Lilly

TO THE INGENIOUS LOVERS OF ART

We have formerly some thoughts of revising our Introduction to Astrology, now out of print, and to have enriched it from another edition with the choicest aphorisms, both from the writings of the ancients and our own many years' experience, but the laboriousness of that work, considering our age and many infirmities of body, with the discouragements we have already me with from some ungrateful persons, caused us to lay aside (at least for the present) those intentions.

Yet that we might not be wholly wanting to promote anything that might tend to the advancement of Art and gratification of its painful students, and knowing how necessary the ensuing Considerations of Guido Bonatus and Aphorisms adjoined, are to be known and regarded, which many of our ingenious countrymen could not do, for they have hitherto remained in the Latin tongue with the rest of the works of these authors in large volumes, difficult to be got at and too chargeable for man to buy, we therefore recommend them to a friend to be translated by themselves, which he has judiciously performed in plain significant language, so that we judge the work may deserve the title Anima Astrologiae which we have given it, comprehending the marrow and substance of Astrology, and much excellent matter necessary to be observed by all honest students that practice Art to discover truth and not to vapour with.

We doubt not but the legitimate Sons and well-wishers of Urania will find considerable advantages from hence, directing them to a certainty in giving judgments upon all occasions, and they will for this publication have cause to thank their old friend.

William Lilly
Walton-upon-Thames, 2 August, 1675.

PROEM

Amongst those things that appertain to giving judgment in questions of Astrology, there are six to be considered: - 1st -Nations, and their particular kinds. 2nd Families, and the constitutions and ordinations of Families and Houses. 3rd - Rich and potent persons, Dispositions and affairs. 4th - Regard is to be had to the Individuals of human kind. 5th Elections or times proper for the beginning of any Work or Enterprise. 6th -Questions as well universal as particular, pertinent and fit to be demanded.

But first of all there are some things necessary to be premised: As the fit manner of propounding a question, and divers other points to be observed in diving judgment. Of which sort of considerations we shall reckon up no fewer than One Hundred Forty and Six, which though 'tis impossible they should happen or be so observed altogether; yet they all deserve to be known, and without them an Astrologer shall never be able to give true and perfect judgement. But before we treat distinctly of them it will be convenient to say a little of the right way or manner how a question should be proposed; for to judge of things to come is no easy task, nor indeed can it always be exactly performed; but we may come near the truth, and differ from it only in some small time or circumstances; which difficulty should not at all discourage us from studying and endeavouring to obtain as great a knowledge therein, as Human minds are capable of; for since inferiors are governed by superiors (as all agree), and that the nature and disposition of such superiors may be known by their motions, which arc now exactly found out by the learned in Astronomy; we may thence undoubtedly arrive at an ability of judging of things to come: That is declare what will happen by or from such their motions, and by consequence foretell future accidents; for this art has its peculiar rules and Aphorisms and its end in judgement, which takes off their objection who say that Astrology is nothing worth; for it would not be an Art, unless it had its proper precepts; but that it is an Art, we have sufficiently proved elsewhere, and the same is generally acknowledged; and its end is to give judgements as aforesaid, which are accidents imprinted on inferiors by the motions of the superior bodies and their qualities and effects in or upon the same.

Thou art here presented with two choice pieces of Art in our mother tongue; the first, the Considerations of Guido Bonatus, a person no less happy in the practice than skillful in the theory of Astrology of which I will here give thee one instance as it is recorded by that eminent Historian Fulgusos, That Guido Earl of Mount-Serrant being besieged in that city, our Author Bonatus sent him word, that if such a day and hour he would make a sally on the enemies' camp, he should give them an absolute defeat, and force them to raise their siege and quit the place, but should himself receive a dangerous (but not mortal) wound in the thigh. The Earl providing himself of all things necessary in case of a wound, and according to the prediction, though vastly inferior in numbers, obtained a most signal and entire victory, but following the pursuit was wounded in the place foretold, of which in short time he recovered.

The second, consists of the choicest Aphorisms of Cardanus, a man famous to the learned world, and of whom the judicious and severe Scalier (though an adversary) in the preface to the book he wrote against him, gives a most respective and applauding character. These Aphorisms (by which is meant short comprehensive and approved rules of Art) were in the original delivered promiscuously, but I for better method have taken the pains here to marshal them under their distinct and proper titles, and that I might not unnecessarily charge the reader, have omitted such as seemed trivial or superfluous; this much I thought fit to premise, and have only more to add, that by reason of my absence some faults have escaped the press, besides those which myself may be chargeable with in the translation; the Reader will show his judgment in distinguishing, and his good nature in pardoning them.

Henry Coley
April 29, 1675

THE CONSIDERATIONS OF GUIDO BONATUS

Book One.

1. The 1st, is to observe what it is that moves a person to propose or ask a question of an Astrologer; where we must take notice of three motions: the First, of the mind, when a man is stirred up in his thoughts and bath an intent to enquire; a Second, of the superiour and celestial bodies; so that they at that time imprint on the thing enquired after, what shall become of it; the Third, of the free will which disposes him to the very act of enquiring; for although the mind be moved to enquire, 'tis not enough unless the superiour bodies sympathize therewith; nor is such motion of the stars enough, unless by the election of his will the person does actually enquire.

2. The 2nd consideration is (what we hinted at before) the method or manner everyone ought to observe that enquires of an Astrologer; which is, that when he intends to take an artist's judgment of things past, present, or to come, he should, first, with a devout spirit, pray unto the Lord, from whom proceeds the success of every lawful enterprise, that he would grant him the knowledge of those things of the truth of which he would be resolved; and then let him apply himself to the astrologer with a serious intent of being satisfied in some certain and particular doubt, and this not on trifling occasions, or light sudden emotions, much less on matters base or unlawful, as many ignorant people used to do; but in matters of honest importance, and such as have possessed and disturbed his mind for the space of a day and night or longer; unless in sudden accidents which admit not of delay[1].

3. The 3rd, is to consider how many ways Planets operate upon Inferious Bodies according to the divers Qualities of their motions: there being Sixteen different ways of such their operations and effects in all things that are either wholly or in part perfected or destroyed.

4. The 4th , is to consider particularly these several Sixteen ways, and what are the assisting causes that help forward things to perfection, and what there are that destroy things after they are perfected. Now of these the first

(1) is Profection, or an advance of or in, things, which the philosophers call 'Alchecohol.' (2) Detriment, which they call 'Aliber.' (3) Conjunction or Reversion, which they call 'Alitifall.' (4) Separation, which they call 'Alnichirat.' (5) Translation of light, which they call 'Annecad.' (6) Collection, which they call 'Algemei.' (7) Probition, which they call 'Almana.' (8) Reception, called 'Alcobol.' (9) Being void of course, called 'Gastalcobal.' (10). Permission, called 'Galealocir.' (11). The restoring or giving of virtue or disposition, called 'Alteat.' (12). The withdrawing of virtue, called Dalpha Alchoa.' (13). The withdrawer or driver away of disposition, called 'Daffaredbit.' (14). Fortitude, 'Alcoevah.' (15). Debility, 'Adirof.' (16) is the state of the Moon called 'Gnaymel,' or the Moon ill affected; which the ancients generally hold to be of ill signification.

5. The 5th, is to consider, how many ways the Moon comes to be so ill-affected, which are generally reckoned to be Ten, but in my opinion Seven more may be added, whereby hindrances and damage happen in all Questions, Nativities, Elections, and actions whatsoever; the First is, where

---

[1] NOTE BY LILLY."Those that take this sober course, shall find the truth in what they enquire after; but whosoever do otherwise, deceive both themselves and the artist; for a foolish Querent may cause a wise Respondent to err, which brings a scandal upon Art amongst inconsiderable people, whereas the Astrologer is not blameable, but the ignorant silly Querent."

the Moon is combust, that is to say under the Sun's Beams, which is counted from 15 degrees of the body of the Sun as she applies to him to 12 degrees distance from him as she is separating from him; and the impediment is greater when she is going to the Sun than when she is going from him; because as she goes off, when she is got five degrees distant, she is said to be escaped, though not wholly freed. As when a fever hath left a man, he is said to be recovered, although he be weak and faint, because he is secure now that he shall obtain his health again. The 2nd is when she is in the degrees of her descensions, that is in the 3rd degree of the Scorpio, or in any part of Scorpio or Capricorn or injoined with any planet that is in her or its own descensions, as if she be joined with the Sun, who is in Scorpio or Capricorn or in any part of Scorpio or Capricorn or injoined with any planet that is in her or its own descensions, as if she be joined with the Sun, who is in Scorpio or Capricorn or in his proper descension, viz., in Aquary or Libra, viz., in its 19th degree or in any part of Libra; or should be joined with the Mars, and he be in Libra or Taurus, or in the 28th degree, or in any part of Cancer; and so with any other Planet or Planets respectively. The 3rd is when she is posited in any of the combust degrees, of which the worst are: those 12 degrees which are before the degree which is directly opposite to the degree in which the Sun is, wherever she shall happen to be, The 4th is when she is in conjunction, opposition, or square to either of the Infortunes, Saturn or Mars, without a perfect reception; for with one it hinders but little, but in all other places 'tis a grand impediment, both in the said aspect and also in corporal conjunction save only where the Infortune shall have two of his smaller dignities, as with Saturn in the 4 last degrees of Aries or Gemini, in each of which he has a Term and a Triplicity; or with Mars in the last 10 degrees of Pisces, where he has a Face and a Triplicity; and so in any other sign or place. The 5th is when she is with the Dragon's Head or with the Dragon's Tail, that is, within twelve degrees of either of them, because that is the place where she is eclipsed. The 6th is when she is in Gemini, which is the twelfth from her own House. The 7th is when she is in the end of the Signs, which are all Terms of the Infortunes, except the last 6 degrees of Leo, which belong to Jupiter; but in the first eight she is weakened because they are in the Terms of Saturn. If it be objected by the same reason she must be impeded likewise in the first 6 degrees of Cancer, since they are terms of Mars, I answer no, because Cancer is her own House and greatest Fortitude. The 8th is when she is in the 6th, 8th 9th or 12th Houses (not in reception with the Ascendant), or joined to any Planet that is in any of them or posited in the Third House, because it is cadent from angles; yet because the same is said to be her joy (or that she delights therein), she is not afflicted there so much as in other Cadent Houses. The 9th is when she is between the degree of Libra and the 5" degree of Scorpio, which 30 degrees are called Combust Way. The 10th when she is voyd of course, that is, not joined to any planet by body or aspect, or in that condition when they call her Feral or Desart, that is, in a place where she has not any dignity. The 11th when she is slow of course, because then she may be compared to a Planet Retrograde. The 12th when she is in want of light, so that no part or very little of her is seen, which happens about the end of the lunar month. The 13th when she is besieged by the two Infortunes impediting her. The 14th if she be in Azimene degrees. The 15th if in Pitted degrees. The 16th if in Smoky Degrees. The 17th and last is when she is posited in those degrees which are called Dark. To know and distinguish all which you have Tables commonly in most Books of Astrologie.

6. The 6th Consideration, Is to regard another manner whereby planets are dibilitated or weakened and afflicted, not much different from the former, which comes to pass Ten ways. The 1st when a planet is Cadent from Angles or from the Ascendent, so that he does not behold the same. The 2nd when the Planet is Retrograde. The 3rd if they be combust, that is, within 15 degrees before or after the Sun; the lower Planets are more debilitated, being behind the Sun, and the less before him, when they are direct; but when retrograde the contrary. 4th When any of them is in Opposition, Corporal Conjunction, or Square of either or both the Infortunes without Reception. 5th when any of them are besieged by the Infortunes, so as to separate from one and be joined to another, without perfect reception of House, Exaltation, or two of the smaller Dignities, which are Term, Triplicity and Face. when a Planet is joined to another in his Declension or Fall, that is, in Opposition to its own House or Exaltation. 7th when it is joined to a Planet Cadent from the

Ascendent, or separates from a Planet that did deceive him, and is joined to another that doth not. 8th when a Planet is Peregrine, that is, in a place where he bath not any Dignity: or being one of the Superiours is followed by the Sun, or being of the Inferiours when it follows the Sun. 9th when a Planet is with the Head or Tail of the Dragon, without Latitude. 10th when a planet weakens itself, that it, when it is in the seventh house from its own, Freal, or not in Reception. These are the Impediments of the Planets, that cause Hindrances, delays, and mischiefs in Nativities, Questions, Elections, etc.: all which thou oughtest to be well acquainted with. There are some more that seem necessary to be known, but to avoid tediousness and confusion I shall at present omit them.

7. The 7th Consideration, is to beware of those cases wherein the Astrologer is subject to err and mistake; of which the learned have named four: 1st When the Querent is so silly that he knows not how to ask, nor what he would have. 2nd When the time for which the figure is erected is mistaken. 3rd When the Artist knows not whether the Sun be gone off the line of the Mid-Heaven, or still upon it: or be behind or before it. 4th When the Fortunes and Infortunes shall be of equal strength; at which time thou therefore oughtest not to receive any question. But, in my opinion, there mat well be added yet three ways more, wherein the Astrologer will subject to err: When the Querent comes only to try him, or put a trick upon him, as many do, saying, 'Let us go to such an Astrologer, and ask him such a thing, and see if he can tell us the truth or not.' Just as the Jews propounded questions to our Lord Jesus Christ, not so much to be resolved, as to tempt and ensnare Him. 2nd Wherein the Artist will be liable to err, is when the Querent does not ask out of a serious or settled intention, as some do when they meet an Astrologer by chance or go to him on other business: on a sudden they think of something, and so ask, as it were by-the-bye; wherein 'tis a thousand to one but mistakes happen. But thou mayest be ready to say, 'How shall I know whether the Querent come out of a solid intention, or only to try me?' To which I answer, that it seems a very abstruse and difficult point, perfectly to find out; but this I have often experienced and found true, viz., I observed the hour of the Question, and if the Ascendant then happened very near the end of one sign and beginning of another, so that it seemed as between both; I said they did not ask seriously, or that they came to try me; and I have had many that have there upon confessed what I said to be true, and began to think that I knew more than before they believed. For in such cases I used to say, 'Pray, friend, do not trouble me unless you ask seriously, for I suspect that you would put a trick upon me, by not proposing this Question as you ought: however, if you will give me trouble for your pleasure, be pleased to give me likewise satisfaction for my pains'; and immediately, if there were and deceit intended, away they went. Another, viz., a way whereby an Astrologer may err, is when the Lord of the Ascendent and the Lord of the Hour are not the same, nor of the same Triplicity, or be not of the same complexion with the Ascendant; for then the Question is not Radical, as I have frequently found by experience. And this I have recited, that thou may'st know for what persons thou shouldst undertake to give judgment; for as one says, "The issue of the thing is according to the solicitude of the Querent, and as he comes in necessity, as sad, thoughtful, and hoping, that thou art able and knowest how to satisfy him the truth of the matter; and in such cases thou may'st securely venture upon the question."

8. The 8th Consideration is, to mind how many of the aforesaid manners or points necessary to be used and heeded in giving Judgments thou hast to consider; and they are Thirty, that is to say, sixteen impediments of the Moon, ten of the other Planets; as hath been said, and besides all those the Planets' several joys, which are four. Of which the 1st is the House which each Planet does delight in, as Mercury in the Ascendant, the Moon in the Third, Venus in the fifth, Mars in the sixth, the Sun in the ninth, Jupiter in the eleventh, Saturn in the Twelfth. The 2nd is, when a Planet is in a sign he delights in, as Saturn in Aquarius, Jupiter in Sagittary, Mars in Scorpio, Sol in Leo, Venus in Taurus, Mercury in Virgo, and the Moon in Cancer. The 3rd is when Diurnal Planets, as Saturn, Jupiter, Sol, and Mercury, are in Diurnal Houses in the East and Oriental of the Sun near the Horoscope; and the Nocturnal Planets, as Mars, Venus, Luna and Mercury, are in Nocturnal Houses in the West and Occidental of the Sun; especially near the cusp of the seventh. The fourth is when the three Superiors, Saturn, Jupiter or Mars, are in Masculine Quarters; which are counted

from the cusp of the Tenth House to the cusp of the Ascendant, and from the cusp of the fourth house to the cusp of the seventh house; and when the Feminines, viz., Venus or the Moon are in Feminine Quarters, which are from the cusp of the Ascendant to the cusp of the fourth house and from the cusp of the seventh to the cusp of the tenth. As for Mercury, he delights when with Masculine Planets in Masculine Quarters, but with Feminine Planets in Feminine.

9. The 9th Consideration is to take notice of the several ways, as well secret as manifest, good and evil, whereby things are helped or hindered to be done or not done, and of these there are one and twenty in number. 1st a most strong secret helper. 2nd A very strong secret Helper. 3rd A strong secret helper. 4th A weak secret Helper. 5th A weak secret Helper. 6th A most weak secret Helper. 7th A most strong manifest Helper. 8th A very strong manifest helper. 9th A strong manifest Helper. 10th A weak manifest Helper. A weaker manifest Helper. 12th A most weak manifest Helper. 13th A most strong secret Hinderer. 14th A very strong secret Hinderer. 1 5th A strong secret Hinderer. 16th A weak secret Hinderer. 17th A weaker secret Hinderer. 18th A most weak secret Hinderer. 19th A most strong manifest Hinderer. 20th A very strong manifest Hinderer; and 21st A strong manifest Hinderer. All which we shall treat particularly, the same being a secret of secrets. In the judicial part of Astrology which the ancients did not regard, nor have said anything plainly of it that I find, save only that 'Haly' seems to have touched a little upon it in his Exposition of the 23rd of Ptolemy's Centiloquium; nor do I believe they omitted those things out of ignorance, but rather through disuse or fear of being too tedious, or burdening the minds of their Readers or Auditors; For they were wont to judge, according as they found the Planets disposed in Houses and Signs, their Fortitudes and Debilities, together with the Part of Fortune, and some few other things. But thou oughtest to consider in thy judgments, not only what they did, but also all other circumstances that thou canst; for when thou dost erect a figure, thou should'st first fine the Significator of the thing enquired after, or to be undertaken, and see if any of the fixed stars of his own Nature being either of his Houses, or in his Exaltation, or in conjunction with him to a minute; for then such star shall so far help the significator, that the thing shall be accomplished and effected, even beyond the Querent's hopes, and this is a most strong secret Helper: For the Querent may well wonder how it comes to pass. Now, if the same star should be in the same degree with the Significator from one minute to 15' before him or 5' behind him, it will still help him, but not so much: and this we call a very strong secret Helper; but if it be with him in the same degree, but above 16 minutes distance and within 50', it will somewhat help, yet this less; and this we call in the Positive degree only a strong secret Helper. If it be in the same degree with the Significator, in a place where he has two of his smaller Dignities, in the very same minute, or within 16 minutes, it will help him yet less, and then 'tis a weak secret Helper; from 16' to 50' still less, and then 'tis a weaker secret Helper; but if it be with the Significator in a place where he has no dignities at all it will still help, but as it were insensibly; and this we call a most weak secret helper. The like we may say on the contrary of those things that prejudice, frustrate, and hinder business: For if a Planet which is Significator of anything, being in a place where he has not any Dignities, shall be joined with one of the Fixed Stars of a contrary nature, it will weaken him and not suffer the thing to come to pass; although otherwise by the Figure it seemed never so probable; so that, for want of heeding this, the Artist often gets discredit, and raises a scandal on the Art itself amongst the ignorant: and this is a most strong secret Hinderer; whereas if the same Star be remote above 16 minutes from the Significator, it will weaken him, but not altogether so much; whence it may be called only a very strong secret Hinderer. And so downwards through all degrees in the same manner as we said of the Helpers or Assistant causes respectively.

Of the several twenty-one Modes aforesaid, which are most strong Helpers, &c. and which strongest obstructs.

The several Modes before mentioned are thus to be known and distinguished: A most strong manifest Helper or Adjuvant cause, is when the Planet which is Significator of a thing, is in his own House; in an Angle on the very minute of the cusp, direct, swift of course, in reception, and free from all affliction and impediment; which most seldom happens.

A very strong manifest Helper, is when the Significator is in his House or Exaltation in an Angle within a degree or two of the Cusp, free from impediment, and in Reception, which very seldom happens.

A strong manifest Helper, is when the Significator is in an Angle in his House or Exaltation, within 3 degrees before the Cusp, or 5 degrees after it.

A weak manifest Helper, is where a Planet is in two of his lesser Dignities in an Angle within 5 degrees before or 15 degrees after it; or is in his House, or Exaltation, in a succedent House free from affliction.

A weaker open Helper, is when the Significator is in his own House or Exaltation, or two of his lesser Dignities, but in a cadent House of the Figure, yet beholding the Ascendant. A most weak open Helper is when the Significator is in some of his greater Dignities, or two of his lesser, not beholding the Ascendant; or in one of his lesser Dignities; only beholding the same, or joined to a Planet that beholds the same, and has some Dignities therein.

A most strong open Hinderer is when the Significator is in a place where he hath no Dignity, no delight, is not received; besieged by the Two Infortunes, Cadent from an Angle, and from the Ascendant: and so much the worse if joined with any of the Fixed Stars, of a mischievous nature, &c.

There may be other both adjuvant and obstructing causes, besides what we have mentioned, both open and secret: proceeding from the conjunctions of Planets and their Aspects, too tedious here to discourse of. Nor shall I here enlarge on all those before mentioned, but most assure thee that this ninth consideration, carefully observed, will be of great use in raising a true and wary judgment; especially if thou hast always a diligent eye to the Moon; for she of all the Planets has the greatest similitude and correspondence with inferior things, both in general and particular: as well the species of the kinds as the individuals of the species; with winds; to pass by her daily effects which she causes in all things here, and frequent revolutions about the Elements and Elementary Bodies by reason of the nearness of her Orb to the Earth, and smaller circle than any other Planet; so that she seems a Mediatrix between Superiour and Inferious Bodies.

And as we see that in the New Moon she appears small and thin, and little, but afterwards her light gradually increases, till all that part of her body towards us becomes replenished with lustre: and then again it decays by insensible degrees till she totally disappears: just so do all bodies both of things Rational, Irrational, and Vegetative: as men grow until they are completed   to their determinate stature, and then droop and decline continually till their life is ended; and so of all other things.

Hence tis necessary to make the Moon concerned in the Signification of every Question, Nativity, Enterprise and Business, and her good condition to show the good issue of the thing: and so on the contrary. For her Virtue and Power is such and so great, that if the Lord of the Ascendant or other Significator of a business be so weak and afflicted that he cannot bring it about and complete it as he ought: if she be but strong it shall, notwithstanding, be accomplished. For she is the School-mistress of all things; the Bringer-down of all the Planet's influences, and a kind of an 'internuncio' between them, carrying their virtues from one to the other, by receiving the disposition of one planet and bearing it to another. And some have thought that she does this at all times, of which opinion was that Tyrant Cylinus de Romano, viz., That when she separates from one Planet, she takes the virtue and carries it to another,   committing the same to the first that she can meet with. And some have imagined that "Zael" said the same; but his meaning was not absolutely so; for lie believed that the Moon did bear what was committed to her; but if it were not so given or committed to her she could not carry   anything to any; to which I assent: for when the Moon is joined to any planet that receives her,   then that planet commits its disposition to her, who carries it with her and bestows it on that planet whom she first meets with any of her dignities, and not to another: according to that Aphorism, ---"A Planet gives nothing in a place, where he has promised nothing."

10. The 10th Consideration, Is warily to observe what Fixed Stars may either help or hinder the matter in question; for they have oftentimes great power, and lead the Astrologer sometimes into error;

and let the Artist be sure to consider the places of the Fixed Stars, as they are in the present age carefully reduced.

11. The 11th Consideration, Is to take notice of the Malevolent Planets, and what they signify; for Saturn and Mars are naturally bad, Saturn for excess of cold, and Mars for excess of heat; not that either of them is really hot or cold, but virtually so; and these are their effects. And so they signifie evil and damage and hindrance, unless they receive the Significator or the Moon by House, Exaltation, or two of their smaller dignities; or shall themselves be Significators; for then they will bridle their malice, and not weaken or hinder him whom they receive, with what aspect soever they behold him; but if they do not receive, their malice is increased; and so much the more if they be in opposition or Square; for in Sextile or Trine the mischief is less. Yet 'Zael' seems to say that Infortunes lay aside or restrain their malice, where they are in Trine or Sextile; but his meaning was only that they were not then so violent, and intended not that their malice was wholly abated.

12. The 12th Consideration, Is to behold the Fortunes, and see what they signify; for Jupiter and Venus are Fortunes by Nature, and being temperate, are said to be without any malice, because they do hurt to none, unless now and then by accident; which is beside their intention and profitably, and always endeavour to help both their own and others, whether they receive them or not; but so much the better if they receive them; and their Trine or Sextile is better and more advantageous than their Square, and their square than their Oppositions.

13. The 13th Consideration, is to regard the Sun and his Significators, for he is also called a fortune, and so, whatever aspect he shall be beheld by, unless it be Opposition; but by Conjunction he becomes an Infortune, because he then renders every star that is so in Conjunction with him, combust and unfortunate; unless the same shall be in the heart of the Sun, and there every star is fortified.

14. The l4th Consideration, is to mind Mercury and the Moon, and what Planets they are joined with; because they will have the signification with those with whom they are so joined; being of a convertible nature.

15. The 1 15th Consideration, is to regard the several ways in general whereby Planets make impressions on these inferior things, which are two, one good and the other bad; for the Fortunes have power of imprinting good naturally, and the Infortunes as naturally slower down ill impressions; whence thou mayest, wherever thou seest the Fortunes, hope for good; and when thou beholdest the Malevolents, fear mischief, unless the same be restrained as aforesaid.

16. The 16th Consideration is to take notice whether the Planet is Significator of anything, be afflicted by either of the Malevolents; which is when one of them cast his rays upon the rays of such Significators, according to the quality of their Orbs; and Whilst he so continues with his rays or light under those of the Malevolent, such Significator is said to be impeded, hindered or afflicted, till the Malevolent have passed him; and 'Zael' says, "After the ill Planet has passed the Planet he did afflict, one whole degree, the Planet shall be said to be freed of him." But rather I think that after the Malevolent is passed him one minute, he may be said to be free and excepted for afterwards he can only frighten him. True it is he raises a greater fear when he is passed him only one minute, than when he is gone by a whole degree; but yet even then it is such a kind of fear as is not altogether without some glimmering of hope. As thus, One intending to go into a Battle, inquires whether he shall return from thence safe and sound or not? And the Ascendant is Gemini 13 degrees, and Mercury in the 7th degree and 54 min. of Aquary, in the 9th joined with Saturn, who is likewise in 7 degrees 53 minutes of Aquary, so that Mercury is now separated from Saturn, who was Lord of the House of Death, one minute; whence it appears that he should have died in that engagement by reason of the Conjunction, and was in peril of death and a kind of desperate

fear that he should be slain by his enemies and shall be pursued by them so that he shall be pursued by them so that he shall seem not able to escape, and they shall often lay hands on him, but at last he shall get away from them and make his escape; even beyond his own hopes; and all because Mercury is separated from Saturn; and 'Zael" saith, "That if a Malevolent planet that would hinder any business be cadent from the Ascendant so that he cannot behold it, he cannot really hinder the matters; but only puts the persons concerned into terrors and frights about it."

17. The 17th Consideration, is to view whether the Planet that is Significator, be safe and prosperous, that is free from any affliction from the Infortunes; and one of the Fortunes casts his beams or light on the beams of such Significator; for then shall that Planet be said to be safe and guarded till the Fortune is passed by the space of one minute, and signifies the perfection of the thing. But after he has passed him one minute, it will not be perfected or accomplished; for it only raises hopes; as (we said) the malevolent in the like case could do nothing, but create fear. Yet is such a hope as the Querent will believe and fancy himself as it were certain; yet not without something of doubt; as for example, A Question is proposed of some weighty and

difficult business, whether it will be done and brought to pass or not? And 17 degrees of Scorpio Ascends, and Mars is 12 degrees 13 minutes of Taurus, and Venus in 12 degrees and 14 minutes of Capricorn, so that Venus is joined to Mars by a Trine, and receives him in her House, who likewise receives her in his Exaltation; so that the Querent thinks, and all others concerned verily believe, that it would be accomplished by that aspect of perfect friendship; in which flattering hopes they continue till Venus hath passed the Aspect of Mars one whole degree; but at last the business comes to just nothing at all, because Venus was past Mars one minute at the time of the question proposed. Yet may a thing possibly in such a case be brought to pass, but not without extraordinary labour and trouble. And here likewise 'Zael' affirms, "That if the Fortune be cadent from the Ascendant, so that it cannot behold the same, it only flatters with splendid hopes, but never completes the business."

18. The 18th Consideration, Is to take notice when a planet is in the Angles of the Infortunes, for unless these receive him there, he shall be said to be in an ill condition, and in straits and troubles; as a man on whom some have made an assault; who has many to combat with and none to assist and take his part; or like one that strives against the stream, or falls into a deep pool, and knows not how to swim; and yet by trusting out his hands and feet, may obtain the bank and escape; though this seldom happens. Now a planet is said to be in the Angles of a Malevolent, when the Malevolent or Infortune, viz., Saturn or Mars, is in one sign, and the other Planet in the fourth, seventh or tenth from him: as if Mars be in Aries, and Mercury in Cancer, Libra, or Capricorn, he is said to be in his Angles: understand the like of their Corporal Conjunction. But if there be Reception, he does not afflict; for reception abates all malice, as we have said elsewhere.

19. The 19th Consideration is, To behold the Moon if she be 'void of course,' for then it signifies an impediment to the thing in question, it will not come to a good end, nor be accomplished; but the Querent shall be forced to desist with shame and loss.

20. The 20th Consideration is, To observe whether the Moon or Significator be joined to any of the Planets, for thence you must derive your judgment of what is like to happen in business. Take notice therefore whether the planet to which the Moon or Significator joins, receives them; for then there will be good laudable end; and the matter will be accomplished with success, if the receiver be a Fortune. But if there be no reception, yet if the Moon or Significator shall give virtue to that planet, the thing will still come to pass. But if it be an Infortune, though they do not give him virtue, yet without a reception it will not do; but with a reception, if he be not afflicted, it signifies a good end of the matter, though not without much labour and tediousness.

21. The 21st Consideration is, To see from what planet the Moon separates: for that signifies what is past of the business: as from a Fortune the good, for an Infortune the ill that hath been.

22. The 22nd Consideration is, To note which if the planets the Moon is now joined to, for that signifies what is now present; and from thence we must judge of the present state of the matter.

23. The 23rd Consideration is, To behold to whom the Moon is now joining [or by applying aspect], so as her conjunction is not yet completed: for that signifies what is to come: wherefore if thou wouldst judge of a thing, which as yet is not, but 'tis hoped will hereafter be brought to pass, 'tis necessary then thou shouldst see to whom the Moon will next join; and according to her signification judge whether good or evil.

24. The 24th Consideration is, To note whether the planet who is significator, be in his Declension, for then it causes a hindrance to everything thereby signified, and trouble and grief about it; and if the Question be about a prison wherein the Querent fears he shall be put, it signifies he shall be cast into the same together with disgrace and prejudice; and if the Question concerns one already in prison, it signifies confinement and more affliction than he believes.

25. The 25th Consideration is, Whether the Planet that is Significator be Retrograde, or Stationary to Retrogradation: for then it signifies mischief and damage, discord, contradiction, and going backward with damage; yet being stationary, is not so bad, as being Retrograde. For the last notes the mischief to be, as it were, present and in being. But being Stationary notes that 'tis past and over.

26. The 26th Consideration is, Whether the Significator be in his Second Station, that is towards Direction; for that signifies also hinderance and evil, which already hath been and is past; yet some say that this Second Station is as good as direction: but this is only a way of speaking, as when one hath been sick and begins to grow well, we say he is recovered and sound, which is not simply true, but somewhere near it; for as the First Station is not so bad as Retrogradation, so the Second Station is not so good as direction.

27. The 27th Consideration is, Whether the Infortunes are the Significators of anything; for if they signify ill, the evil will be much augmented, and if good it will be much diminished, abated, imperfect, and with difficulty; so that the party will scarce think his business done, unless by chance they be in a very good condition and excellently disposed.

28. The 28th Consideration is Whether the Significator be slow of Course, for then it delays the effect; and if it be in the beginning of anything, retards it, so that it will be scarce ever be finished: besides, things proceed slowly, where Significators are pointed in Sagittary, Capricorn, Aquary or Pisces: or who are the Lords of them, whether they be slow of Course; in Aries or Scorpio they are not quite so dilatory. In Leo they hasten business; more in Taurus or Libra; but most of all in Gemini or Virgo.

29. The 29th Consideration is, Whether the Moon be joined to any planet by body or aspect exactly to a minute; for that signifies the present state of things; and from that minute observe what planet she joins next, for he shall be Significator of all that shall happen of that thing; as the planet she was last before with, was of what has already passed as aforesaid.

30. The 30th Consideration is, To observe when a planet that is Significator, or the Moon, shall have past the 29th degree of the Sign wherein it is, and touches the 30th , and especially if it have passed one minute of that degree; for then it shall have no strength in that Sign, but in the next; so that if in the first it signified any evil, it shall hurt the person or thing threatened no more than the fall of a house shall one that is just got out of it; or being with one foot upon the threashold, has one behind him that throws him out; and then the building falls. And if it signifies any good, it shall profit no more than he that hath spread a nest for birds, and just touches the feathers of their tails,

but never catches their bodies; and therefore 'Zael' says, "If a planet or the Moon be in the 29th degree of any Sign, its virtue is yet in that Sign wherein he is; because he has not yet wholly past the 30th degree." &c.

31. The 31st Consideration is, To look when one planet applies to the Conjunction of another, if he be near the end of the same Sign wherein he is himself, or that other to whom he applies; so that he will pass out of that Sign before the Conjunction is perfected; and to see if he be joined with him in the following Sign to which he is changed, because then the cause is perfected; if that planet confers anything on him in that Sign wherein he is so joined to him; that is, if any Reception happen, unless the said planet, or he to whom he applies, be first joined to another; for then the business comes to nothing, and will not be perfected, though he be joined again to the other interposed before the first conjunction is accomplished. Nor must it be forgotten that a Corporal Conjunction forbids an Aspect and cuts it off, but an Aspect cannot do so by a Conjunction.

32. The 32nd Consideration is, If an Infortune be the Significator, what his condition is; for if it be good, there will good come of the thing; if bad, rather evil; as 'Sarviator' says in "PENTADERA," "An ill-planet strong in his own Home or Exaltation, Not joined with any other Infortune to impede or weaken him, is better than a Fortune Retrograde afflicted."

33. The 33rd Consideration is, To see whether either of the Infortunes be the Significator of anything, and be joined to another Infortune impeding him, or has joined to him the Lord of the Ascendant or the Moon, by a square or Opposition; for then this Infortune will perfect the business, but the business will not be good, or rather it will be destroyed after it seems perfected. But if the Infortune that Impedes be the lighter of the two, so that he apply to a Conjunction, with the Significator, it will hinder less than if the Significator apply to the other.

34. The 34th Consideration is, To mind in Questions or Nativities, whether the Significator of the business be an Infortune and Lord of the Ascendant, and in the Ascendant; direct, not vitiated, and in good condition; for then he would both affect the same and bring it to a good conclusion; nay, although he be not Significator nor Lord of the Ascendant, but only be in the Ascendant, and that the same be his Exaltation; he lays aside all his malice, and is restrained from mischief; but if he be weak and afflicted, his malice and contrariety is increased so as to destroy the business wholly.

35. The 35th Consideration is, To look whether an Infortune be in Signs like him, or of his own nature, for that abates his ill effects; like a cross fellow when he is pleased and has what he will, as Saturn in Capricorn, Aquary, or Libra, or in a cold Sign, especially if he have any dignities there: and so Mars in Aries, Scorpio, Capricorn, or a hot Sign, &c. But if Saturn be in a hot Sign, or Mars in a cold Sign, out of their dignities, it will be bad, and the business be no more completed, than oil will mix with water; but if strong and well disposed, they will mix in good, like water and wine, or milk with honey.

36. The 36th Consideration is, To observe when the Infortunes are the obstructors of a business, whether the Fortunes behold them with a Trine or Sextile Aspect; for then their ill-nature will be allayed and mitigated; but much more if these receive them.

37. The 37th Consideration is, To look is the Fortunes are the Significators? Whether the Infortunes behold them with Oppositions or Squares; for that will much lessen their kind effects, and diminish the good they otherwise promised.

38. The 38th Consideration is, To consider if the Fortunes are Significators, whether they are Cadent from Angles, or from the Ascendant, so as not to behold the same, and be Retrograde; for under these Impediments they will be almost as bad as the Infortunes themselves, unless they be in reception.

39. The 39th is, To consider if the Significator be in Reception; for id it be a Fortune, its signification will thereby be much bettered, and its impediment and mischief much lessened   if it be an Infortune.

40. The 40th is, To consider if an Infortune, whether he be Significator or not, be Peregrine; that is, not in any of his Dignities, for then his malice is increases; but when in his Dignity it somewhat abates it; that is in his House, Exaltation, or Terms; but in his Triplicity or Face very Little, and in Hayz least of all.

41. The 41st is, If an Infortune, being Significator, be in his own House or Exaltation, or in his own Terms or Triplicity, or in Angles or Succedent Houses; for by all these means he is fortified, and shall be counted strong as a Fortune.

42. The 42nd is, If a Fortune be Significator, or give virtue or assistance to any of the Planets, and be in a house where he has none of the Lordly Dignities, then his good signification will be lessened and abated; and so on the contrary.

43. The 43rd is, If the Fortunes and Infortunes be together il-posited, that is, in some of the said Impediments, as Houses where they have no Dignities, Combust or the like; then whatever they signify 'tis but weakly; according to that Aphorism of the Philosopher, "A Planet Retrograde and Combust, has no strength in Signification. The Fortunes when Combust and under the Sun 's beams, signify none or very little good; and the Infortunes in like case have little or no virtue to signify ill." [An unfortunate should be regarded as having very evil signification under the circumstances.]

44. The 44th is, To consider if the Significators, Fortune or Infortune, be in his own House, Exaltation, Triplicity, Terms or Face (but the latter being not of that virtue with the rest, 'tis necessary it should be assisted with another Dignity, which is Hayz or Light); for in such   case the Infortune loses his sting; and being rein'd in like a wild horse from doing mischief, his malice is converted into good, and though this seems strange, yet the ancients affirm and   I myself have often found it true by experience.

45. The 45th is, To consider if the Infortunes are in angles of the Ascendant, that is, in such signs as are in Square or Opposition to the Ascendant, when they afflict any Planet by Square or Opposition; for then they assist so much the worse, and do more mischief, especially if they be in a stronger place than such afflicted Planet; but if they cast only a Trine or a Sextile, it is lessened and the Impediment mitigated.

46. The 46th is, to see whether the Significator be a Fortune or Infortune, the first naturally signifies good and prosperity, the last naturally evil by its malignity; therefore consider the Planets' places from the Ascendant where they are; for if a Planet be in his Light, or his Hayz in any of his Dignities, or in a good place from the Ascendant, it signifies good, and if it be a good planet the better.

47. The 47th is, To consider whether the Significator be in his Light or no, that is a Diurnal Planet in the day, above the earth, and in the night under the earth; and a Nocturnal Planet in the night above the earth, and in the day under it; for this renders such a Planet more strong. But if a Nocturnal Planet be Significator of anything in the day above the earth, or a Diurnal Planet in the night, the same is thereby weakened and under a kind if impediment, that he   can scarce accomplish what he signified.

48. The 48th is, To consider, when an Infortune is Significator and his ill effects are mitigated, whether Jupiter behold him, or is joined corporally to him? For that will wholly destroy his malignity and turn his nature into good, how bad soever he be; so that if Saturn in that place of himself would not bestow some good or perform what he seems to promise, Jupiter will make him do it, provided he be not afflicted himself, as in his fall, Combust or Retrograde (yet even then he helps, but not so powerfully). On the other side Venus takes off the fury of Mars, by reason of that endearing intimacy which is between them, unless the thing be very difficult, as wars and bloodshed, &c. But she cannot so well divert the mischief of Saturn without the help of Jupiter (and then she can do it as well as at other times that of Mars). The reason is, there is no such sympathy between Saturn and she, in any respect; for he is slow. she swift; he heavy, she light; de delights in melancholy, she in mirth.

49. The 49th is to consider, Whether one of the Infortunes being Significator, be joined to another, for if he signified a good himself, this will destroy or frustrate it; but if any evil, it will augment and double it, or change it into some worse mischief of another of another kind; as when the pain near the navel turns into a dry Dropsy; but if joined to a Fortune with a Reception on either side, the evil will be converted into good; but without a Reception it will only be allayed and abated, according to the strength of such Fortune.

50. The 50th is, To observe the Lord of the Ascendant and the Moon, whether they or either of them are afflicted by either of the Infortunes, by Conjunction, Opposition, or Square, the business will be spoiled without the aspect of a Fortune, but if the Fortune, that is, Jupiter, Venus, the Sun or Moon shall behold them, it slackens and dissolves the rigours of such Infortunes, and the party signified shall be freed from the danger impending, although the aspect be a Square, provided it be with Reception:

but if a Fortune without Reception, by a Square or Opposition, or an Infortune with a Trine or Sextile without Reception, shall behold the said Lord of the Ascendant, 'tis possible the party maybe delivered from the present danger; but it will be turned into another as great: so that it will not profit him.

51. The 51st is, To see whether the Significator be cadent from an angle or from the Ascendant, and in none of his Dignities, nor in his Joy; for then he signifies nothing but doubts and mischief, and there are no hopes of good or profit from a planet so disposed.

52. The 52nd is, When the three Inferiors, Venus, Mercury, and Luna, come from under the rays of the Sun, and appear in the evening after his setting, for before (viz., till they are got from him 12 degrees) they, or any other planet, are weak, so that a Fortune can advantage little, and an Infortune prejudice as much. Now if the Fortune come forth slow in motion, as with labour, then will not the good expected be obtained without much pains and trouble; and if it be an Infortune, his signification will appear slowly. But in the Superiors, as Saturn, Jupiter, and Mars, these things happen when they come from under the Sun beams, that they rise in the morning before the Sun, and shine before his rising.

53. The 53rd Consideration is, Whether the significator be under the Sun beams, for then he will be of small efficacy in anything as aforesaid; yet the Malevolents will be something more strong in evil than the Benevolents in good[2].

---

54. The 54th is, To consider whether a superior planet be removed 12 degrees from the Sun, going to his morning rising, or an Inferior is so much, and direct, going to his evening rising, for then he is said to be fortified; but when he is got 15 degrees, so that he appears, he is more fortified in everything: like one coming out of a battle rejoicing having destroyed and outed all his enemies. But when the Sun follows the three Superiors, and there shall be between them and him less than 15 degrees, their weakness is said to be increased, until there shall be only 7 degrees between them and afterwards, until they shall be in the heart of the Sun, they are said to be in extreme debility; but the debility of the Inferiors is contrary to them, for it is said to be increased when they follow the Sun, and that there is between them and the Sun from 15 degrees to 7 degrees, and from 7 degrees till they are in the heart of the Sun, they are said to be in their greatest debility.

55. The 55th is, To consider whether the significator be Peregrine, for then the person whom he signifies, either in a Nativity or Question, &c., will be subtle, crafty, malicious, one that shall know how to act both good and evil, but more inclinable to the latter.

56. The 56th is, To consider if the significator of anything shall commit his disposition or virtue to any other Planet? Whether it be to one that is Oriental or Occidental? For if he be Oriental and one of the Inferiors and direct, or if he be Occidental and one of the Superiors, and that there be not above 20 minutes between him and the Sun, he will be weak says 'Sarcinator,' and not perform what he shows, but hinders many things; under that impediment like a sick man whose disease has prevailed so far, that he is forced to lie by it, and cannot help himself; or a falling house which none can preserve from ruin; and so much further as such Planet shall be from the Sun, so much less shall he be afflicted. And if it be Oriental, and one of the Superiors, or Occidental, and one of the Inferiors, and not Retrograde, he shall be strong and fit to perfect what he promises; as one that hath been ill, but is more perfectly recovered, or a building which fell and is repaired, and so of all other planets so disposed.

57. The 57th is, To consider whether the significator be in the Eighth from the Ascendant? For if he be there, and a Fortune, though he do not harm, he will do no good; and if he be an Infortune he will do greater mischief than in any other place of the Figure; and if the Question be of going to War, advise not the Querent to go there, although it be a Fortune; for always some evil is to be suspected, that is death, or at least captivity, for it is a place of darkness and death; but if it be an Infortune, judge death, unless he separate then from the Lord of the Eighth; for then it may be only a wound, or bruise, or a fall, wherein he was in danger of death, although he may escape; and if it be a journey, especially a long one, he will be taken prisoner, or in great dread of it; understand still if he separate from the Lord of the Eighth; and also remember that an Infortune so disposed always does more mischief than a Fortune.

58. The 58th is to Consider, Whether the Significator be fixed in that Sign where he is found? Now 'Zael' saith: "That a Planet is not said to be fixed in a Sign till he hath passed 5 degrees thereof." But I am of the opinion that when he hath passed one whole degree of a sign he is firmly therein, but he said it for more certainty. So likewise he says: "That a Planet is not said to be cadent from the Ascendant, unless he be removed from thence 5 degrees; as, for example, the Ascendant in 9 degrees of Aries, and a Planet was in the 5th degree thereof 'Ptolemy', and many other sages affirm, That Planet to be in an angle, with whom I agree; yet some would have it, that a Planet should be said to be in an angle, when he is in the very degree of the Ascendant, or one degree before it or two after it; but they meant in Revolutions, and that they might be so certain as not to be in the least deceived. But I have experienced that a Planet is in an Angle to the space of 5 degrees beyond the cusp; for as once I sought the Revolution of a year, I found Mars in the 5th degree beyond the cusp of the angle of the earth in Capricorn, South Latitude, which signified the killing of the Roman Emperor; and acquainted him with it, for his court at 'Grossietti' and I at 'Forlirii'; and it was found that 'Pandulfus de Farsenella' and 'Theobaldus Franciscus', and divers others of the secretaries had conspired to slay him, and none of his own Astrologers observed it,

because they did not believe that Mars was in an Angle, for he was 4 degrees beyond the cusp and 58 minutes in their opinion; however, after a Planet shall be removed from the cusp or line of any angle full 5 degrees or more, he is to counted Cadent from that Angle."

59. The 59th is to Consider, Whether the significator be behind the cusp of an angle 15 degrees and no more; for he shall be said to be in an Angle as well as he that is exactly there, as 'Zael' affirms; whence he said before that it was not in an Angle, nor had any strength there beyond the 1 5th degree after the cusp of the Angle: For example, the Ascendant is 4 degrees of Taurus, and the end thereof was behind the Angle, whatever planet is posited from the 4th to the 19th degree thereof is in the angle, but what is beyond that is not; but Ptolemy seems to imitate, though he says not expressly, "that every planet who shall be 5 degrees before, or 25 degrees after the cusp, is in the Angle." Now 'Zael' would clear the doubt, lest that great distance of the planet from the Angle should hinder the business.

60. The 60th is to Consider, Whether the significator be in a Sign fixed, common, or moveable; because in a fixed Sign he signifies stability and countenance of the thing begun, or to be undertaken, or enquired of, In a common Sign, a change with a return or repeating of it, that the same will once be broken off, and afterwards begun again, or something added, or other alteration happen; for which reason in things that require alteration, as buying, selling, or the like, we should put the Significator and Moon, or one of them, into a common sign, but in a moveable Sign it signifies a sudden change, a quick despatch or end whether good or evil. And therefore in matters where we desire a sudden conclusion, we ought to put the   Significator in moveable Signs; but things that we desire should be fixed and endure, we ought to place them in fixed Signs, there we would have a mean, let them be in common Signs, understand the same always of the nature of the Moon, if at any tine that canst observe it.

61. The 61st is to Behold, Whether the Lord of the Ascendant or Moon, be with the Dragon's Head or Tail; for that is an impediment in all affairs, and the hindrance or mischief wilt proceed from a cause simplified by that House the Dragon's Head or Tail hurts, unless it be corporal for they have no Aspect or Opposition. And it is worse when the Significator or Moon goes towards them, than when they go from them; for in the first case is signified the mischief in its full height, like a man in a ship that is split in the sea, when there is no hope. But in the last, 'tis like a ship that is only in danger, but has hopes and probabilities of escaping. And note that when the significator or Moon goes to the Dragon's Head, its malice is augmented, for its nature is to increase, and when they go to the Tail, the mischief is not absolutely at the worst, as 'tis when they go from it, that is, within one degree; for from one degree forwards 'tis not so great as in that degree, although much; and from 1 degree to 3 degrees less, and from 4 degrees to 5 degrees yet less, and from 5 degrees to 7 degrees very small; from 7 degrees to 9 degrees smaller, and from thence to 12 degrees little or nothing at all.

62. The 62nd is to Consider, Whether the Moon be void of course? For that signifies that the thing enquired after shall scarce ever come to a good end, and not without much labour, sorrow, and trouble, unless the Lord of the Ascendant or significator of the thing, shall be in very good condition, and then it may be hindered, but not wholly frustrated; yet 'tis a good time then for drinking, bathing, feasting, &c., and to use ointments for taking away of hair, especially if she be in Scorpio.

63. The 63rd is to Consider, Whether the Moon be far from the Conjunction of the Infortunes, so as not to cast her beams on theirs, for then the event will be good, but rather if she touch with her beams those of the Fortunes. And yet better, if besides this the Lord of the Ascendant, or of the business, be in good condition; for if they be not well disposed, it may impair the good promised, but not wholly prevent it.

64. the 64th is to Consider, Whether the Moon be in Cancer, Taurus, Sagittarius, or Pisces; for it signifies good in the business, although she be joined to the Infortunes and not to the Fortunes; nor does she, being void of course, prejudice so much in those places as elsewhere, provided she be not Combust, for then they will advantage her little or nothing.

65. The 65th is to Consider, Whether the Lord of the Seventh is afflicted or not? For that will be an impediment to the business. And you ought to defer judgment if you can, and warily search always whence such impediment shall arise, as well by the Conjunction of the Lord of the Seventh with the Planets, as by their separation, and also of the Moon; so may'st thou find whence it will proceed, and afterwards give judgment with more safety.

66. The 66th is to Consider, When the Infortunes threaten mischief, whether the place on which their threats fall, be the Dignity of any of the Fortunes? And whether such Fortune behold the same place by Trine or Sextile? For then it will take away the mischief and annul it wholly. If by a square, it will only lessen it; if by an Opposition, take away some part of it; but if it cast no aspect at all, the mischief will happen; but it will proceed from honest, just, persons, and it will be the Querent suffers rightfully, being cast in a just cause before a Judge, or the like. But if the aforesaid place be the Dignity of an Infortune, the prejudice will come from unjust men, false witnesses, a corrupt Judge, or some sentence unjustly given through a mistake, &c.

67. The 67th is to Consider, Whether there by any Eclipse near, which is less than 12 degrees from the Significator? For the same will bring damage and mischief to the Querent or business, unless there be a Fortune which hath Dignities in the same place, for then the same is abated; but if there be no such, thou oughtest to look what Planet beholds the said place of the Eclipse and how. For if the Fortunes behold it, they do but augment the evil; and if they are Infortunes, they lessen and abate it, which seems a kind of riddle or wonder in Art.

68. The 68th is to Consider, In questions relating to sick people, or Decumbitures, Whether the Lord of the Seventh, and the Seventh House itself, be free from Impediments? For if they be, the sick may safely trust himself to the care of the Physicians, for medicines will do very well. But if the Seventh House and its Lord shall be Afflicted, Ptolemy saith "The Physician must be changed, for neither his physic nor care will do any good"; for the seventh signifies the medicine as 'Zael' saith; or at least the disease grows chronical and lasting. The like is to be expected if the same positions happen at the beginning of any cure.

69. The 69th is to Consider, Whether the significators of the Ascendant, and of the House signifying the thing enquired, be of equal strength and debility? For then thou canst not safely give judgment: but in such case thou must mind the Lord of the Conjunction or Prevention (as the thing is either conjunctional or preventional) which was last before, and by that judge, but if the Lord of the Conjunction or Prevention, and of the things, be still equal, thou must then turn to the Moon, and see to whom she first applies, and thence deduce judgment. If she join not to any in or from the Sign in which she is, take that with whom she joins first in the next Sign, and this is very considerably useful.

70. The 70th Consideration is, To mind another secret; not well searched into by Astrologers, but often times doing them much prejudice; that is, see in all Questions, etc., whether the Lord of the New or Full Moon, preventional last before, be in any of the Angles of the thing enquired after; if it be, it denotes that the business will be accomplished, unless it be the Querent's own fault (or that God overrule against it),though perhaps by other significations it seemed not likely. But if it shall not happen so but only the same is in the Ascendant; and the other significators that is, The Lord of the Ascendant of the thing enquired of and the Moon, or any of them assist, the thing well be done with ease. If it be in Cadent Houses, it will scarce ever be, though other significators seem never so favourable; and if two at least of them be not so, take it for certain it will never be done.

71. The 7lst is to Consider whether the Significators falls between the Ascendant and the Twelfth, for that signifies continuance or length of time, when a thing will be done; or if done already, how long it will continue in days or hours. If between the twelfth and the tenth, it notes half-weeks; between the tenth and seventh, months or weeks; between the seventh and fourth, years; and between the Fourth and the Ascendant, half years.

72. The 72nd is to Observe, That if the question be of a journey, and the Moon afflicted, it is not safe to undertake it; but if it cannot be put off, make the Planet that afflicts her, Lord of the Ascendant at the time of the Querent's setting forth.

73. The 73rd is to Mind, Whether the Questions signify good or evil? If good, whether the Fortunes behold the Significator of the Question, or the Moon? For then the good Fortune thereof will be increased: but if the Infortunes cast their beams, as much or more diminished. But if it originally signify evil, and the Infortunes behold the Significator or Moon, as aforesaid, the evil threatened will be increased and becomes much worse.

74. The 74th is to Consider, Whether the Significator be in his first station, going to be Retrograde? For that signifies crossness and disobedience, and that the matter, though never so probable, will not be accomplished. If any work or building be then begun, it will not be finished. And if such Significator, so asserted, be then under the earth, such building shall not be raised to any purpose in thirty years, and then not finished; and if it be raised a little then, it will be a raising thirty years more. And if not then completed, it will not be completed till ninety years after its first; and if not then, it will never be finished, unless the property be altered, and come into the possession of strangers from its former owners. But if the Significator be in his second station, going to be direct, it notes that the affair will be done, but slowly, intricately, and with pains and trouble. And if an edifice be then begun, it will be finished; not so soon as was first believed, provided the Significator be not under the earth; for then he that begins it shall never make an end of it, nor raise it very high above the earth[3].

75. The 75th is to Consider, Whether the Moon be afflicted by any Planet? For then, whatever the question be, the same will suffer impediment. But if the Moon be in a good place from the Ascendant, so as to behold it with a Trine or Sextile, or if the Planet that afflicts her do behold the same. Either of these Aspects will mitigate the mischief intended, and it may be, wholly take it away, as the said afflicting Planet is disposed; so that he be not Cadent from angles, nor from the Ascendant, nor in his fall; that is with the seventh from is own House. 'Zael' seems to say That is an Infortune afflicting be cadent from the Ascendant, or Retrograde, it causeth fear in the Querent; but I always fear the affliction of the Moon above all other Impediments, and scarce Remember that I ever saw a good end of anything where she was afflicted and in journeys, if to war, was apprehensive of the Querent 's care and person; if for traffic, of straits, quarrels, sadness in his travels, and loss of money, &c.

76. The 76th is to Consider, From what Planet the Moon separates, and which she is joined to; he whom she separates from signifies what hath been, the other what is to come, as we have said. And therefore, if she separates from an Infortune, and applies to a Fortune, the worst is past; and what hitherto has been had, will end happily to the Querent's content. But if she separates from a Fortune, and goes to an Infortune, understand the contrary, the thing was good in the beginning, but proves naught in the end. If from a Fortune to a Fortune, is was and is good, and will have a

---

[3] NOTE BY LILLY: "And note A Planet in his second station signifies an aptness, and the renewing and strength of everything; but in his first station, dissolution and destruction. Remember and understand these thing well, for they will often come in practice."

laudable end. If from an Infortune to an Infortune, it will be an ugly conclusion. [This Consideration is in the doctrine of 'Translation.' Translation of the light and nature of a planet when a planet separates from one that is slower than itself, and overtakes another either by conjunction or aspect. In horary astrology it is a good omen if the aspect be good; but if by an evil aspect, it is said to denote evil or difficulty when the event comes to pass. Thus, if a question of marriage a light planet translates the light of the lord of the 7th House to the Lord of the Ascendant, it is a good omen, if it be by good aspect, and denotes that a person answering the description of such translating planet will bring the parties together, and they will be eventually happy. If it be by evil aspect, it will be done either from ill motives or will be attended with much trouble and disappointment.

77. The 77th is to Consider, Whether the Lord of the Ascendant or Moon be in Opposition, that is, whether the Moon be in Capricorn, Mercury in Sagittarius or Pisces, or Venus in Scorpio or Aries, the Sun in Aquarius, Mars in Taurus or Libra, Jupiter in Gemini or Virgo, Saturn in Cancer or Leo; for then such Lords of the Question abhor the business; nor does he love it should be accomplished, but is rather against it.

78. The 78th is to Consider, The House that signifies the thing whereof the Question is asked. For the First signifies the Person, the second, substance, the third, brethren, etc., as we have before taught, and as it shall appear, so judge; having duly pondered all circumstances.

79. The 79th is to Consider, Whether the Significator, or Moon, be joined to good or ill planets, by Conjunction or by Aspect, which is diligently to be heeded and distinguished; for a corporal conjunction with the Sun is the greatest misfortune can befall a Planet.

80. The 80th is to Consider, How the Significator is posited in respect to his own House, whether in the second, third, or fourth, &c., sign, from it, according to the Signification of that sign shalt thou judge, as thou wouldest judge of any Planet in such an House from the Ascendant.

81. The 81st is to Consider, Whether the Significator be in an Angle or in a Succeedent or Cadent House? For how much any Planet is near to the cusp of any Angle so much is he the stronger: how much farther so much the weaker; and by how much sooner he shall be nearer the cusp of a Cadent House, so much shall he be the weaker; how much the farther, so much the less weak.

82. The 82nd is to Consider, Whether the Significator receive disposition or virtue from any Planet, Fortune or Infortune. If from a Fortune it signifies good; and the better if such Fortune be in a good condition. If from an Infortune, to the contrary; and so much the worse by how much the more weak and afflicted he is.

83. The 83rd is to Consider, Whether the Fortunes and Infortunes are equally strong in the Question: for that signifies no positive judgment, either good or ill; but a kind of indifferency, and that the business will bring neither gain or loss.

84. The 84th is to Consider, Whether the Fortunes or Infortunes are strongest; for if both be strong, and the Fortunes prevail in strength, it signifies a kind of mediocrity of good; if the Infortunes in such a case are strongest, a mediocrity of evil not in excess on either side.

85. The 85th is to Consider, Whether the Part of Fortune fall in a good or bad place of the Figure; that is in an Angles, or in a Succeedent or in a Cadent House; and how the same is aspected, and by whom, a Fortune or an Infortune? And whether it be in reception of that Planet by whom it is aspected? For questions may sometimes seem good but the Part of Fortune happening in an untoward Place, weakens it much and renders it less profitable so as to deceive the Querent's hopes. And on the contrary a question may seem ill, yet the Part of Fortune happening luckily,

joined with a good Planet that receives it, &c., lessens the evil, and not so much happens to the Querent as the Figure otherwise seems to threaten.

86. The 86th is to Consider, Whether either of the Infortunes behold the Significator both Retrograde, Cadent, Peregrine, and in signs contrary to their respective natures? For then they bring such an absolute mischief as cannot be avoided, nor averted by anything but God alone. And if any shall be born under such positions, he will always be a beggar, let him do what he can; if any House be built then, no man shall ever live happily, or get money in it; but by losses and crosses his estates and goods shall moulder away, and come to nothing; and his most probable designs strangely frustrated and destroyed, unless the Divine Goodness in mercy interpose.

87. The 87th is to Consider, Novenarium Lunae, which is a thing much to be heeded, for it often hinders the Astrologer from discovering the truth, and leads him into error, not knowing the cause that makes him deceive.

88. The 88th is to Consider, The Planet from whom not only the Moon separates, how he is disposed, &c., but the next to whom she is joined, so that there be not above 51 minutes distance between them, the first signifying what is past, the second what is now present, as we have already said, and also look to whom she will next be joined after separation from him with whom she is at present; for he will signify (according as he is disposed) the issue, or what is to come.

89. The 89th is to Consider, The Duodenariam Lunae, a thing that is observable in many cases, even more than divers things that we have said; for there is greatest danger of mistakes in abstruse considerations, and such as Astrologers rather sloth than ignorance, do not regard; whereby they often fall into disgrace and contempt of the rabble, rather than take a little pains.

90. The 90th is to Consider, Whether the Lord of the House in which the Sun is, and of that wherein the Moon is, and also the Lord of the Ascendant be all oriental and in Angles (though that rarely happens), and mutually behold each other from good places with friendly Aspect; for these positions shall signify the greatest good, and most superlative future imaginable. If they shall not be all so disposed, the remaining part shall signify prosperity and felicity proportionally as far as they are able, though not in so vast a measure.

91. The 91st Consideration is, To observe in Questions or Nativities, whether Mars be in any of the Angles of the Figure, especially in Fixed Signs; or when Scorpio Ascends, for then he destroys all the good signified by that question, or at least much impedes and diminishes it; Unless Jupiter behold him with a Trine or Sextile; for then his malice is mitigated; but yet as Jupiter is either strong or weak.

92. The 92nd is to Observe in Nativities and Questions especially of death, whether the Lord of the House of Death, or Significator of Death, Lord of the House in which the Lord of the Eighth is posited, applies to the Significator of the Native or Querent, or he to them; because a Planet so affected becomes the destroyer of Life, and kills as well if it be a Fortune as an Infortune, and that whether there be a Reception or not.

93. The 93rd is to Consider, If the Question concerns a thing that one would desire of another, or that one would get out of a secret hidden place, whether the Significator of the Querent, or thing inquired after, behold Saturn or is corporally joined to him; or whether Saturn be in the house of the thing inquired after? For then the business will hardly be done, or not without much labour and trouble, and more tediousness than the Querent can imagine.

94. The 94th is to Consider, In Questions, &c. whether the Significator of the thing inquired about be Cadent from the Ascendant, or other Angles, or from the house that signifies the thing or business

sought after, or its Lord? Or whether he be Retrograde, or in a bad condition with the Sun, or whether there be in the said house, signifying the thing inquired after, a Planet Cadent, or Retrograde, or in such ill condition with the Sun, or in an ill place from him, or ill aspected by him; for any of these things signify a hindrance to the thing, although otherwise the Question seems good and probable.

95. The 95th is Whether the Planets signifying the thing sought, join mutually with each other; for that signifies it will be done; yet, be not too confident to judge so, till thou hast well weighed the nature of the sign wherein they are joined, whether it be of their own nature; for then it will be easy, otherwise difficulty; or scarce at all.

96. The 96th is to Consider in Questions which seem to show, that what is enquired after shall be perfected, whether the Significator of the thing, and the Moon are in Angles; for if they both be above 25 degrees from Angles, it will not be accomplished; but if one shall and the other shall not be so far off, then it may be done but with difficulty, unless it be a journey; which will speed well enough if the significator be remote from Angles.

97. The 97th is to Consider, in what climate thou receivest the Question; for judgment must be varied as the ascensions of countries and climates differ, there being not the order in the ascensions or elevations of signs, in one climate as in another, nor the same Ascendant in one region as in another[4].

98. The 98th is to Observe, Whether if what appears by the sign likely to be effected, be signified by the planets by corporal conjunction, or aspect or translation of Light? If either of the two, first the thing will be effected by the Querent, and the party enquired of, without any third person intermeddling; but if by the last it shall be done by ambassadors, friends, or some person interposing himself; and it shall be brought to pass by a person or thing signified by that House whose Lords translate the lights as aforesaid. Thus if it be the Lord of the second, it will be done by expenses, or a piece of money; and if by the third, by some brother or the like; if by the fourth, by the Father, &c., according to the respective signification of each House.

99. The 99th is to Consider well In Questions, Nativities, &c., what will certainly come of them; for sometimes by the Figure, a thing seems likely to be absolutely done; but is not wholly, but in part; sometimes it is wholly perfected, and sometimes neither wholly nor in part: upon which account astrologers are often blamed, and scarce know how to excuse themselves, not knowing how this comes to pass, being a difficult point, and of a most subtle disquisition; so that the ancients would not meddle with it save only the most honoured 'Albumazar' said something more than the rest, whose judgments I have found more efficacious and correct than others, though 'Ptolemy', the

---

[4] NOTE BY LILLY.'Beware therefore of a mistake here, for it will be very unhandsome and blameworthy; for whatever part thou travellest towards, from one region to another, whether from the East to the West, from the North to the South, or contrarily, your Ascendant will be changed from one degree from East to West in Longitude and e contra, and from the North to South, and the contrary. But some jocund fools or monks, in their cups, may arise and say, If your judgments are changed according to the situation of Nations they are false. But there is no talking to such brutes, they neither understand nor believe, nor is anything probable to them: Yet there are some very learned men amongst them, such as 'Contradus Brixiensis, 'a preaching Friar, who excellently understands Art and practiseth it honestly. Want of heeding what I have said hath made Astrologers to err, and I doubt doth so still, for right judgments cannot be given but by the Ascendant and other Houses, and therefore, if these vary, those must do so too. Therefore you should have Tables of Elevation for every Climate and Region; yet 'tis more difficult to find out the difference of one climate from another, than of one Region or country from another, according to the Longitude; for if thou hast tables of the elevation of the signs in any region from East to West, thou mayst by guess find the elevation in another, which way thou pleases!, either towards the East or West, according to the same climate, by taking the difference, but in divers climate thou canst not so easily conjecture."

great explainer of this science, must be acknowledged more curious than the rest. Now that which I say is the consideration of certain Fixed Stars:

100. The 100th Consideration is, To observe the Fixed Stars assisting and promoting the accomplishment of things, which are thus situated. In Aries there are two, one in 5°06', of the nature of Jupiter and Venus, another in 26°0l' of the nature of Jupiter. In Taurus three, one in the l°03', another in 8°07', and the last in 9°0l', all of the nature of Venus. In Gemini are two stars one in 19°02', the other in 21°08', both of the nature of Jupiter and of the second magnitude. In Cancer likewise two, one in 2°02', the other in 29°05', both of the nature of Jupiter. In Leo one in 9°04', of the nature of Jupiter and Venus. In Virgo one in 4°07', of the nature of Jupiter and Moon. In Libra two, both of the nature of Jupiter and Venus, one in 13°45', the other in 14°45'. In Scorpio four, one in 9°55', another in 13°01', a third in 14°45', the last in 19°15', all of the nature of Jupiter. In Sagittarius two, one in 10°15', the other in 7°55', both of the nature of Jupiter. In Capricorn three, one in 2°03', another in 7°55', both of the nature of Jupiter. In Pisces two, one in 7°11' of the nature of Venus, the other in 14°59' of the nature of Jupiter. Wherefore always when thou findest the signification in a corporal conjunction with any of these, thou mayst pronounce happiness and a good end.

101. The 101st Consideration is, To mark in Nativities or Questions, which Planet is the cutter off of life or years, or hinderer of a thing from being done; for he it is who destroys the life of the Native, &c., who is strongest in testimonies of dignities or power. Yet Messabala concealed this, and discovered the secret only to a certain scholar of his, who out of pride appropriating the same to himself. Now after thou hast found who is this destroyer, &c., then see to whom the Lord of the Ascendant or the Moon is joined (who participates in signification of everything, as we have said before), or the Lord of the thing enquired after, and the Lord of the house of the Moon, or one or more of them; for if it be joined to a planet Retrograde or Combust, or cadent from the Ascendant, or any other Angles, or to any of the   Infortunes who doth not receive him; or is afflicted by an Infortune, which cuts off the light of the significator: the thing is destroyed, and so the years of the Native are diminished and he lives not long. Further, If the Lord of the Ascendant, or the Moon, or the Lord of the   thing enquired after, be joined to a Planet who is free from the conjunction of the

Infortunes, and so safe as to himself but is joined to another Planet afflicted, some of the aforesaid ways, the matter shall be brought to nought, even after it seems accomplished, and the Native" life shall be suddenly cut off, when there is all the probability that may be of the contrary: and this will also happen though there be no conjunction with the killing Planet, if only the significator or Moon be afflicted in manner aforesaid.

102. The 102nd Consideration is, of things signified, how they shall be found or known, and from what significator they are to be taken? Which must be from the significators of the querent, and of the thing Questioned or enquired after: which two significators, if they shall be joined together with the Moon it signifies wholly and absolutely the effect of the thing; if not joined, then the contrary. And from the conjunction of the significators we ought to know why, or by what the question is made. And by the Lord of the House in which such conjunction happens, we know of what the question will be, or the end thereof~ for if that be a Fortune it will be good, according to the conditions and signification of such Fortune, and the House wherein he is, and signification of the place in which the Lord is posited of that House wherein itself is. But if it be an Infortune, it will be bad, according to the signification of the Infortunes, and such other positions as aforesaid. If the Lord of the House or Exaltation, or of any two smaller Dignities, casts an aspect, or there be a translation of light, you may know by that the question shall be brought to pass: but if there be none of these it cannot be precisely known, but it will be by or from a cause not yet discovered: and by the aspects of the fortunes or Infortunes may be known what will be the effects.

103. The 103rd Consideration is, To mind in Nativities and general Questions in what House the Part of Fortune happens; for from the things signified by that House will the Fortune or gain of the Native or Querent arise, if the same be well disposed, otherwise the same will be cause of his misfortune and loss.

104. The l04th Consideration, To observe in Nativities and general Questions whether the significator of the Native or Querent be posited in the Seventh from his own House, or the Opposition to the Lord of the Ascendant: for be will not in such case signify gain from the things signified by that House, but rather expense and loss.

105. The l05th Consideration is, To observe in Nativities or general Questions, whether that an Infortune, unfortunate be in the Seventh? for that signifies that the Native or Querent shall not live in peace or any delight with his wives, sweethearts, or companions, but will perpetually have brawls and quarrels with them: it seldom happens otherwise from such a position.

106. The l06th Consideration is, To consider in Nativities and general Questions, it a Fortune fortunate, and in no way afflicted be in the Seventh? for then the Native or Querent shall be happy in good wives and associates, yet shall have many rivals and persons that hate him, but rather out of envy than cause, so that he shall seldom bring his enterprises and designs to pass, without much labour and trouble.

107. The 107th is, To consider in Nativities and general questions, whether Mars be in the Second or in the Tenth, and well disposed; for it denotes that the Native or Querent shall gain a Fortune or Estate by those persons that deal or work in Iron and Fire, as Smiths, Furnacemen, Glassmen, etc.: or in Victualling or keeping Inns, Taverns, etc.: but if Mars be weak or afflicted, loss and damage from all those.

108. The 108th Is To Consider, If neither of the Planets beholds two Houses? For his virtue and fortitude shall be in that wherein he hath most dignities, and which is most proper for him, and the thing he signifies.

109. The 109th Is, To consider whether the Lord of the Fifth be in the Seventh afflicted? For then the Native will never be happy at Feasts or Banquets; either be averse from or slighted at such meetings, or some affront put upon him; never be happy at Feasts or Banquets; either be averse

from or slighted at such meetings, or some affront put upon him; nor will he ever go neat in his clothes, nor get any credit by them.

110. The 110th is, To consider in Nativities, whether Scorpio ascends? For such a Native is never like to get any great preferment in the Roman Church: because Cancer (the Exaltations of Clerks (priests, parsons, &c., &c), will then be in the Ninth House, which signifies the Church, and Jupiter is an enemy to Mars, who is Lord of the Ascendant.

111. The 111th is, to consider in Nativities and Questions especially of Lawsuits and controversies, whether the Dragon's Tail be in the Seventh? For that signifies damage or overthrow to the Native's enemies and prosperity to the Native or Querent, because the Dragon's Head will then be in the Ascendant. If it be in the 8th it denotes the decay and loss of their estate or substances, and increase of the Native's. In the third, prejudice to the Native's brethern. In the fourth, to the Parents. In the fifth, to his children. In the sixth, to his servants. In the ninth, to his journeys. In the tenth to his preferment. In the eleventh, to his Friends. In the twelfth, to his cattle of the greatest sort, &c. and so to all other things signified by each House respectively: so do Saturn and Mars also, but not so much. Likewise 'tis observable that other ill positions may make void the said significations, but not so much as Saturn and Mars, unless they themselves are significators of the mischief, and then much of their malice is abated.

112. The 112th is strictly to examine and regard in every Nativity or Question, the Ascendant; for whosoever shall have 'Virgo' ascend and Mercury in good condition, or at least not afflicted; if he study and practice Physic he shall have success and do great cures, but shall be unhappy in his salary or profit thereby; not being able to get his fees of most of his Patients; and besides, shall be unhappy in Lawsuits. But if he follow the law, he shall be unfortunate in all his business, and slighted; his words, though never so prudent, not regarded, no not by them for whose advantage he speaks, but a fool's discourse preferred, and whatever he meddles in shall turn out untoward, and people be his enemies without cause, and asperse and scandalize him, but they know not why. But far otherwise will it be if Sagittarius, Taurus, or Pisces ascend and Jupiter, Venus and Mercury, shall be in the Ascendant, or if Jupiter and Venus shall happen to be in 'Zaminium, or the heart of the Sun, whatever the Ascendant be the native shall be admired as a Prophet, and all his words received as Oracles, or the distates of destiny.

113. The 113th Is To Consider, Whether either of the Infortunes be in the IXth House, and with out Dignity? for then the Native or Querent shall be often blamed and accused, and that without cause, as much as for one, But if a Fortune be there well affected (especially having Dignity there) he shall on the other side be praised, applauded, and honoured, whether there be cause or reason for it or no.

114. The 114th Is To Consider, Whether the Lord of the Eighth be a Fortune, and in the Second? for then the Native or Querent shall gain considerably by the goods of people deceased, of his enemies, and by his wives, especially if such planet shall be free from Impediment or have Dignities there. But if an Infortune be there, it signifies loss and decay of the Native's estate, unless he have dignities there and be otherwise well affected, and in good condition, for then it will be little or no prejudice; but without dignities, and in an ill state, it wholly and totally destroys and ruins all hopes of estate.

115. The 115th Is To Consider, Whether the Eighth House, or it Lord be afflicted? For then shall the Querent or Native be damnified, and lose an estate by the death of a wife, which she enjoyed for life or the like.

116. The 116th Is, To Consider which of the Houses, or their Lords are afflicted, or under impediment? For that signifies that hurt and damage will accrue to the Native, by reason of the things signified

by that House; and soon the contrary, if they are Fortunes, good and advantage from tile same things.

117. The 117th Is To Consider, If the Dragon's Tail be in the Fourth; for that signifies, that whatever the Native or Querent shall get shall be squandered away, and come to nothing; and wherever it is, it signifies damage to the Native in and from that House represented.

118. The 118th Is, To consider in what House a Fortune shall be fortunate and strong, well disposed, and not afflicted; for in and by these persons or things by that House signified, shall the Native or Querent gain profit, and make his fortune; and so on the contrary of a House that is afflicted.

119. The 119th Is To Consider, If the Lord of the second be in the seventh, and the Seventh be in Aries, Scorpio, Capricorn or Aquarius; for then the Native's enemies shall easily take away his goods and right; and if he associate himself with persons,. they shall rob him: and his wife or mistress shall cheat him, and steal whatever she can from him: unless the Lord of the Ascendant be in Trine or Sextile to the Lord of the Seventh, or in other aspects with reception.

120.The 120th Consideration is, To observe whether the Lords of any of these Eight Houses, viz., the 3rd, 4th, 5th, 6th, 9th, 11th, or 12th, be in the 7th ? for whichsoever of them is there, the person by him signified will prove the Native's enemy, unless a perfect reception, with some good aspect as Trine or Sextile intervene. Yet a Square or Opposition with Reception will abate the enmity, but not wholly prevent it. Thus if it be the Lord of the 3rd, his Brethern will prove his enemies; if the 4th, his Parents; if of the 5th, his Children, &c., nor shall he gain of or by them so much as he shall lose another time; or if any of them sometimes appear kindly, it will be but from the teeth outward, and for their own ends, &c.

121.The 121st is whether the Moon be in the 8th and the Lord of the Ascendant in the Ascendant; 2nd, or 12th, Retrograde? For then the Native or Querent will not be fortunate, nor have any luck at playing at dice or any other gaming.

122.The 122nd is, Whether the Part of Fortune be in the first 10 degrees of the 4th House, with the Dragon's Head, the Moon, Venus and Jupiter, and they direct? - for that signifies that the Native shall be lucky in discovering and finding out hidden treasure. If it be in the second 10 degrees, or but with two of the said Planets, he shall find some, but not in so great quantity. In the last 1-degrees, and with but one less, and yet a considerable parcel; and if only the Part of Fortune be there not afflicted, then a small quantity. If the Sun behold it with a Trine or Sextile, it will be Gold uncoined; if the Moon, Silver; if Jupiter, a mixture of Gold and Silver, &c. If Venus, precious stones, Lockets, and for the most part Women's Ornaments. But if they be Retrograde, he shall discover the treasure, but not for himself, another shall get the profit. If the Lord of the 8th behold the Lord of the Ascendant with a square or Opposition, the finder shall die by reason of it; but if it be with a Trine or Sextile, he shall only catch some small disease or sickness. If the Dragon's Tail be there instead of the I-lead, he shall find it, but it shall be taken from him; he shall find it, but it shall be taken from him; or being ignorant what it is, he shall give it away almost for nothing; and if the Moon be then separated from the Lord of the Ascendant and joined to an Infortune that afflicts her, he to whom 'tis so given shall have little profit by it. If Mars or the Lord of the Eighth behold the Lord of the Ascendant, they that take it from him shall kill him. But if Mars and Saturn shall be in the place of Jupiter and Venus, the business will be only brass or copper or lead, and if the Lord of the Ascendant be with them, the discoverer is wearied with it, whatever it be, whether vile or precious.

123.The 123rd Consideration Is, To observe in Nativities or Questions? Whether the Sun and Moon are in Conjunction in one and the same minute, both according to Longitude and Latitude, and any of the Fortunes in the Ascendant that is within 15' above the cusp thereof, or 24' below it; for that signifies that the Native shall be happy in getting a great estate and heaping up of money; but if they be only in exact Conjunction to Longitude, and not according to Latitude, and their distance one from the other be within 15' he will still be fortunate in acquiring substance; but so much the less, by how much the further such distance is and so proportionately. If they happen to be above 15' distance, the same thou mayst conclude if the Moon shall be in the very minute of opposition to the Sun, and a Fortune be in the seventh, which signifies the estate of the Querent or Native in respect of his wives, companions, or enemies. And if at that time of birth Taurus ascend, and the Moon be there, or the very minute ascending, or Leo ascending, and the Sun in the minute ascending, and not afflicted by either of the Infortunes, it signifies that the Native shall get much money, and come to great preferment and honour; but either of the Infortunes be in the said places instead of the Fortune, it denotes loss and destruction of estate to the Native or Querent by or on the occasions aforesaid.

124. The 124th Consideration Is, To regard in Nativities and Questions, the Significators of the Querent's and Native's estate and also of his preferment, calling or profession; which thou mayest take to be the Lord of the Tenth, or of the Ascendant, if the other shall not be fit to signify the same; for if the Lord or Almuten of the l0th be with the Light of Time or erect and tall from it, and distant 60 degrees or upwards even to 90 degrees ; if it be one of the Superiors, or 30 degrees if it be on of the Inferiors, and in the Angle of the Tenth, or in the Ascendant within 30 minutes above the cusp, or a degree and a half below it, and not afflicted: it signifies that the Native shall attain to the Dignity and profession of his Ancestors, and not exceed it, yet shall be more skillful, excellent, and perfect therein than any of them; but if there be in either of the said Angles any of tile aforesaid helping and fortunate Fixed Stars with the Planet of Fortune or any of the Planets, he will far surpass his forefathers in dignity. And if such Fixed Stars shall be of the first Magnitude and sole Significators, the Native or Querent shall be raised to cast honours and riches, almost inestimable: which if beheld by the Lord of the Ascendant, then his fame and honour lies in his own Person; if by the Lord of the 2nd, in his riches; if by the Lord of the 10th in his offices, command, or empire; and this though in never so poor and vile people; the meaner their condition was, to so much the greater height shall they arrive. But this shall not endure long, for they seldom go beyond 27 or 30 years. And look, how much the more sublime was their fortune, by so much the more grievous, miserable, and calamitous shall be their fall; for they shall die an ignoble filthy death, or if they escape it, the same shall happen to their next successor.

125. The l25th Consideration is, To observe in Nativities or Questions what sign ascends: if it be the sign of a Planet that hath two Houses, the exercise of troubles of the Native or Querent shall be chiefly in those things signified by the other House of the said Planet, which shall lightly happen to him and for the most part through his own means. As if the Ascendant be in Aries, he shall be excused in those things as shall be in the cause of his own death or fall because Scorpio the other House of Mars will be then in the Eighth House: but if Mars be well disposed and the Part of Fortune happen in the Eighth he shall be very fortunate in all things signified by that House. If Taurus ascend he shall be exercised in those things as shall cause his own weakness, because Libra   which is the other House of Venus will be then the Sixth House. But if Venus be well disposed, and   Part of Fortune in the Sixth, he shall be most lucky in things appertaining to the Sixth House. If the   Ascendant be in Gemini he shall be exercised in such things as shall occasion his being taken; because Virgo, Mercury's other House, will be on the fourth; but if Mercury be well disposed and   Part of Fortune in the fourth, he will be prosperous in things belonging to the Fourth House. If Virgo ascends, he will be exercised in things that will gain him honour and power, because Gemini,   Mercury's other House, is in the tenth. If Mercury be then in Conjunction with the Part of Fortune   and in the Ascendant, he shall acquire as it were a King's revenue. But if Mercury be in the tenth   with the Part of Empire, fortunate and strong, he shall undoubtedly obtain a Kingdom or supreme   command; and if this Part of Fortune and the Moon be also in the Tenth, he will be a mighty Prince   infallibly. If Libra ascend, he shall be exercised in things that shall hasten his own death, because Taurus the other House of Venus will be then in the Eighth. But if Venus

be well disposed and the Part of Fortune in the Eighth he will be lucky in things represented by the Eighth House: and so of any other sign. Scorpio ascending the Native or Querent shall bring diseases on himself because Aries is the sixth. Sagittarius ascending, he shall fool himself into captivity because Pisces is on the Fourth. Capricorn ascending, he shall gain much by his industry, for Aquarius is then on the Second House. But if Saturn be ill disposed he shall squander away and waste his own substance idly. If Aquarius ascend he shall procure himself many secret enemies. Because Capricorn will be than in the Twelfth House. If Pisces ascend, he shall raise himself to honour, etc.

126. The 126th consideration is, To take notice in Nativities and Questions, whether Mercury be significator wholly or in part, fortunate and strong and in Capricorn or Aquarius? For then the Native shall be of profound and piercing wit, and great understanding; one that shall dive into the bottom of things, and see from the beginning what the issue will be; and so much the more if Saturn fortunate shall behold Mercury with a good aspect, especially if Mercury be in Aquarius, which is the delight of Saturn; and still more if a Fortune shall be with Mercury, and he with one of the propitious Fixed Stars. But if Mercury be in Aries or Scorpio, the Native will be bold, Perfidious, inconstant, arrogant, and yet quick of apprehension; rather nimble to repeat or find out things said by others than invent them himself.

127. The 127th Consideration is, To observe in Nativities, if the Lord of the Ascendant be Saturn or Mars, and sole Lord of the Nativity, without any Fortune partaking in the dominion, the taste or smelling of the native or his complexion shall not be like those of other men, for if it be Saturn he shall delight in sour or insipid things, as 'Halion Otolemy' avers; if it be Mars, in sharp and bitter, flesh half stinking, wine dead, and pallid aloes, snuffs of candles, dung, etc., as also with filthy, dirty, unhandsome women; more than in others; or if it be a woman, in the homeliest men, &c.

128. The I28th Consideration is, In Nativities, whether the Ascendant be a human sign or the Lord of it in a human sign? For that signifies the native an honest, sociable, and neighbourly man, more especially if both happen together. But if the Ascendant carry the similitude of some creatures which men use to labour with, as Aries, Taurus, the last part of Sagittarius and Capricorn, the Native is very submissive and humble to men, yet very sociable. But if it be a sign half-feral, as Cancer and Pisces, he will be yet less sociable; but if it be feral, furious or salvane sign, as Leo and Scorpio, he will be of a brutish temper, delighting in the woods, hunting and living upon spoils and rapine; caring not to associate himself with men, so that he seldome remains long with his own Parents or nearest Relations.

129. The 129th Consideration is, To observe in Nativities, whether the Moon be in Opposition to the Sun, with any of the stars called "cloudy" which are 'Althazaic', and the "Head of Gemini,' or in a place called 'The Place of Falling into the Water,' which Aquarius spouts forth, or the drops of the Lion, said to be near his heart, and others which by reason of their mixture with each other do not shine distinctly (nebulous stars). For when the Moon shell not be above 10 minutes' distance from them, according to Longitude and Latitude, it seems unavoidable that the native shall have diseases in his eyes; not to be remedied by any human help or medicine. If the Moon be then Occidental in an Angle and Mars and Saturn likewise Occidental, not far distant from her, or opposing the Sun in any of the Angles: it signifies that the native shall be blind of both eyes at his death; nor does there appear any way whereby it may be prevented; but if it be not of luminaries, but only one, he shall lose but one eye, and if it be Sol and a man the right eye, if a woman the left eye: but if it be the Moon and a man, the left eye; but if a woman, the right eye.

130. The 130th Consideration, is, To regard in Nativities whether the Moon be joined with Mercury by Body or Aspect, or there be a translation of light by any planet between them? If there be nothing of this and the sign ascending be neither of the nature of Mercury or the Moon; and Saturn in a diurnal nativity and Mars in a nocturnal, and one be in an Angle, the native will be mad, distracted,

troubled with fits, a fool or at least exceedingly forgetful, unless a Fortune very strong shall at the same time behold the Ascendant, Mercury, or the Moon; and so much the worse if the Angle wherein such Infortune is, happen to be Cancer, which is the exaltation of Jupiter, or Virgo the exaltation of Mercury, or Pisces the exaltation of Venus. The reason is because the Moon in Nativities is the general Significatrix of the native's Person; and the Planet with whom she is joined of his faculties and powers; and therefore if she be corporally joined or applying to such Planet, the native will prove of good understanding, and very well retain his senses and intellectuals. And if Mercury be in Capricorn or Aquarius, not afflicted, but in good condition, the native will be of an exceeding wit, and a great Philosopher, and if Jupiter and Venus be in (Zamini Solis) he will prove a Hermit or kind of Prophet, whose words shall be received as Oracles beyond those of other men.

131. The 131st Consideration is, To take notice of the Nativity of a man, whether the Sun and Moon be both in Masculine Signs, or both in one Masculine Quarter or one Masculine Sign; for if so, it signifies that the native's acts and temper shall be naturally such as belong to men. But in a woman's Nativity, the Luminaries so disposed, make a kind of Virago, one that shall despise men, and obtrude herself into their affairs; and such a one, if she marry, will be sure to wear the breeches. If Venus and Mars shall be both in Masculine signs, the native will be moderately affected towards the delights of Venus, and use them according to nature and law; but if they happen to be Oriental, he will be more fallacious and immoderate, inclinable to incest, sodomy, etc. But if they be Occidental and in Feminine Signs, his spirits will be nasty and brutish; and so much the more, if Saturn cast any Aspect to them. But if it be a Woman, and Mars and Venus Oriental and in Masculine Signs, she will ebhor men's embracds, and take no delight therein, but rather please herself with some little wantonness with persons of her own sex. But if Mars and Venus be in Feminine Signs and Occidental, she will love and take delight in men's kindness. And Ptolemy in his Centiloquium affirms, That if Venus be joined with Saturn in a Nativity, and have Dignities in the Seventh, the Native shall be somewhat faulty and untoward in his venereal caresses.

132. The 132nd is to mark in Nativities, Whether Mars be corporally joined with a certain Fiery star of his own nature in Taurus, called 'Algol', so that they are not above 16 minutes asunder, Mars applying thereunto and the Lord of the House wherein the Luminary, for the time ruling is pointed, which is called the Lord 'Anaubae'; or of its Exaltation, and two others of its Dignities, and shall be in Opposition or Square of Mars, and neither of the Fortunes shall behold the Ascendant, nor be [pointed] in the 8th House; it undoubtedly signifies the native shall be beheaded. And if Mars shall not be distant from it in Latitude above 6 minutes, it will infallibly happen so; not to be avoided but by God alone. And though a Fortune, Retrograde, or Combust should behold the Ascendant, yet it will scare preserve him from beheading: only in such cases it may happen not to be occasioned by his own fault: for a Fortune in such a case not impedited, may save him from such an ill death, and permit him to die in his bed, but then it will be of some capital disease, proceeding from a hot house, and this before he comes to be fifty years of age. But if Mars shall not be thus affected, yet if an Infortunate be in the 8th, the Native shall come to an untimely or ignominious end; but if a Fortune be there in good state, he shall expire naturally; but if such a Fortune be afflicted, he shall die of some mischance coming upon him[5].

---

[5] NOTE BY LILLY: Ptolemy in his 'Centiloquium' tells us, 'That if the Light of the Time shall happen to be in the Mid heaven (I say in the conditions aforesaid) such native shall be hanged! If either of the Infortunes be in Gemini, and the other in Pisces, his hands or feet shall be cut off according to the signification of the sign wherein the Planet is posited which is most malevolent. If Mars be in conjunction with the Lord of the Ascendant in Leo, and hath no Dignities in the Ascendant, nor neither of the Fortunes in the 8th, the native shall be burnt to death; and ~f Mars be then Retrograde, Combust, or in his Fall, it will be for some crime, otherwise by mischance or unjustly. Ptolemy saith that, If Saturn, in a Nativity, be in the mid-heaven and the Planets to which he is "Aanauba" (a Dispositor) be in opposition to him, and a dry sign on the cusp of the Fourth, the native shall be knocked on the head, or die by some ruins falling on him; but if a moist sign be there he shall be drowned; but if it be an human sign, he will be strangled. If Mars or Saturn be in the Ascendant at birth, and Peregrine, the native shall have a scar or mark on his head or face; if the Infortune be afflicted, Combust or Retrograde, the same will be very deformed, and much disfigure him, otherwise not.'

133. The 133rd consideration is To mark in Nativities, whether Gemini or Sagittarius ascend, and whether its Lord be well disposed, that is, fortunate and strong, and likewise the Moon; for that signifies that if the native live, he will get great riches. If Virgo or Pisces ascend and its Lord or the Moon be well affected, he shall get money and lay the same out well, and live splendidly, being beloved for his generosity and bounty. But in the other case where the Ascendant is Gemini or Sagittarius, he will not be so liberal, but very frugal and sparing; besides, he who hath Gemini or Virgo for his Ascendant may lose his estate and come to want; but he that hath Sagittarius or Pisces shall never lose his means, nor fall into poverty. If Aries, Scorpio, Capricorn, or Aquarius ascend, the native will be miserably covetous. If Jupiter behold the Ascendant, he may somewhat mitigate the sordid humour, but will not wholly prevent or take it away.

134. The 134th is, To mind in Nativities, whether Mars or Venus be in the Sixth, and likewise well disposed? for that signifies that the native shall be not really fit for Physic, and grow a perfect doctor in every part of the Art. If Mercury be in conjunction with Venus and she Retrograde, he will make naturally a good singer; but if Mercury be in the Twelfth not afflicted, he will be studious and famous in most sciences, especially Philosophy.

135. The 135th consideration is, To consider in Nativities, whether the Lord of the Ascendant and the Moon, and Jupiter, and Venus, are either all in the Ascendant, or whether Jupiter and Venus behold the Lord of the Ascendant, and the Moon in the Ascendant by a trifle or Sextile, and free from affliction? for then the native will prove very strong and courageous; and none will dare to disobey his commands.

136. The 136th consideration is, To note in the Nativities of Kings and rich men, and such grandees as are fit to bear rule, whether both Luminaries are in the Degrees of their Exaltations, or in their own Houses, in the dame degree one with the other, and free from affliction? for this signifies that the native shall obtain great honours; for he shall be made Emperor, or something like it; so that he shall be as it were~ monarch of the world, which shall continue to the fourth generation of his posterity. But if all the Planets below Jupiter shall be disposed of by him and he shall receive virtue from every one of them, notwithstanding the condition aforesaid, and afternoon commit both them, and himself to Saturn, and both be Oriental from the Sun and in Angles, the native will be a person of great renown and power, although perhaps not with the title of king; but his fame shall endure for a long time, that is to say , all his lifetime; and after his death from three revolutions of Saturn, or Jupiter.

137. The 137th is, To see whether Mercury be in conjunction with Saturn in the Ascendant? For that signifies that the natives is a foolish talkative fellow, that would be counted wise; he shall speak ill of both men and women; the greatest wit he hath is to invent lies; nor doth he ever open his mouth, but something of untruth appears intermixed with his discourse: so natural it will be for him to tell lies, Saturn give him a foul tongue, and Mercury a sharpness of malice to employ it.

138. The 138th is to see in Nativities, Whether the two Infortunes are in the Fourth House, or whether the Angles are possessed with moveable signs, and Mars and Saturn in them? For then the native will be poor, wretched, and unfortunate, above all others, all his lifetime, unless Jupiter, of the Lord of the Triplicity ascending prevent.

139. The 139th is, To be careful, both in Nativities and Questions, where the Dragon's Tail is? For that signifies the wasting and destruction of the thing signified by that House, especially if it relates to gain, for in the 1st it signifies expenses, and loss of gain to the Querent, from or by reason of his person: in the 2nd, construction, loss by means of Brethern, Sisters, Neighbours, &c.: the 11th, damage that one shall sustain by one's Grandfather, Father-in-law, and such things relating to Inheritances; and that the Native shall change Houses often, and get little by it; in the 5th, damage

from or by reason of children, in the 6th, loss by servants or small cattle; in the 7th, loss by women, Companions, or open enemies: in the 9th, loss by Religious men, and on the account of religion; in the 10th, by or in his preferments, honours, &c.: in the 11th, loss by his friends, or for their sakes: and in the 12th, damage sustained by great Cattle, or by means of hidden enemies.

140. The 140th consideration is, To see whether the Significator of the thing in question, or the Moon be so weak that it cannot bring the matter to perfection? And if they be, take the Significator of the Querent and thing inquired after, and subtract the lesser from the greater, and add to the remainder the degrees of the sign Ascending, and project what they amount unto from the Ascendant, and observe where it happens; for the Lord of that sign signifies what was enquired of and according to his conditions shalt thou give judgment, as thou findest him fortunate and strong, or unfortunate and weak. For if the business concern a man's estate, and he be placed in the Second, as he is; so shall the Querent's estate prove; if in the Third, the Brethren, Neighbours, etc., etc., will be disposed accordingly; in the Fourth, those of greatest Relations; in the Fifth, the Children; in the Sixth, Servants; in the Seventh, Wives; in the 8th Wives' portions; in the 9th , Long journeys; in the 10th , his preferments; in the 11th his Friends; in the 12th , his secret Enemies.

141. The 141st is to consider in Nativities, The gifts and properties bestowed on men by the fixed Stars, and how long they continue, together with the reason why they prove, not lasting as those which proceed from the Planets, since it seems a little probable that they should continue longer that those; of which I do not remember to have met with anything in the Ancients, save only that 'Ptolemy' in his Centiloquim says, The fixed Stars sometimes confer exceeding great benefits; but oftentimes they end will. And 'Almensa' in his Treatise to the Great King of the Saracens, says that the Fixed Stars bestow notable gifts, and raise from poverty to happiness and high degree more than any of the seven planets: Now the reason that the gifts of the Fixed Stars to men, abide with them than those given by the Planets is, because the fixed stars being the Agents, and the men the Patients; the subject on which they are to operate are not agreeable to them, nor are born to be able to receive their impression; for it is requisite that there should be sonic conformity and likeness, or agreeableness between the Agent and the Patient. But the fixed stars are most slow in motion; and   consequently in mutation, whence it comes to pass that their impressions require subjects and patients of the same nature; that is to say, such as are the most lasting, and carry a conformity with them to prefect or accomplish their effects: For the Revolutions of the fixed Stars is finished, but in six and thirty thousand years, but the "Viventhipolis" or life of man, generally exceeds not three revolutions of Saturn: that is to say, the space of ninety years; very few exceed that age, thought possibly some may by the addition of the years of some Planets to the years of the "Alcocoden" in their Nativities, which bears no conformity or proportion with 36,000 years to complete the effects of their influences. And therefore as an Eagle cannot exercise the complement of her flight or power on a Fly, nor a Stone coming forth (a Sundra trabathi) do any great execution (in Musciovem) no more can the Fixed Stars complete the effects of their impressions; and therefore their gifts of the good promised by them continue no longer with men, because men are of so small a duration, and subject to a swift mutability in respect of their Motion. And upon this is that Aphorism grounded, that Advises to make use of fixes Stars in the foundation of Cities, but of Planets in the erection of Houses; because Cities are generally of the longest continuance amongst corruptible things, and far more durable than particular Houses: for these in respect of their individuals do not endure always, whereas Cities remain by a successive building and rebuilding of Houses; and therefore though Castles are very lasting, yet are they not equal in this respect to   Cities; so that although we may use the superior planets in elections for building Castles, it is better to take Fixed Stars; yet still because Cities are of longer continuance than Castles,they are more   appropriated to the fixed Stars, whose Subjects they are. For the impression which a solid thing makes in a more solid thing, continues much longer than that which it makes on a less solid thing; and far less in a thing not solid, than a thing somewhat solid; and yet less in a very slippery transient thing, than in a thing less lubricous or changeable. Hence the impressions which the fixed Stars make on Cities are more correlative to them in length of time,

and accordingly those of Castles more durable than those of Houses, for the same reason proportionally. But bodies of men are more remote from those fixed stars than Houses themselves, and so more corruptible; and for that acause their Significations apply less to them, or if they happen, abide but little; the Significations of the fixed Stars being so great and noble, so high and free from corruption and mutability, that they cannot easily take upon them a variable commixture with things quickly corruptible and suddenly changeable, unless it be as oil on water; for though it may enter into it, yet such impression will not long continue; for the fixed Lights operate with so much nobleness, that by reason of their long distance from those vile corruptible changeable bodies, and neighbourhood to the Supreme Light, their effects cannot remain in or with them, when they are lightly or suddenly changed and corrupted; especially in base people and mean spirits; for they seldom trascend his person to whom they happen, and oftentimes leave him whilst he lives, and that to his damage, so great that Good alone can prevent; as I affirm for the most part; though 'tis possible they may sometimes terminate in good and continue long: As it hath sometimes happened that some have lived to the greatest years of the Alcocoaen, of whom I never say but one in my time, who was named Richard, who affirmed himself to have been a Courtier under Charles the Great, King of France, and that he had lived 500 years. At what time there was a report of one that had continued alive ever since our Saviour's days called 'Johan Buttadeus' because he had impolissed the Lord as he was led to be crucified, Who said to him, "Thou shalt expect, or wait for me, till I come." The aforesaid Richard I saw at Ravenna in the year 1223, and the said John is said to have passed through Florilivium, in his journey to St. James's at Compostella, in the year 1267. Nor could the Significations of the fixed Stars be applied; or adhere to men nor sensibly remain in them, unless there were some Medium by which they might Act upon them which are the Planets, which are secondary Agents, as the first are principal; for whenever there are divers actions in order, attributed to several Agents, the principal act ought to be referred to the principal Agent, which in respect of the effects on corruptible things, was the primary Cause. And the Planets are Secondary: for that corruption which those inferiors suffer, happens by reason of their too great distance from the incorruptible superiors; yet their effects sometime continue long in Grandees, and persons very rich, who are apt for Empire, magnanimous, and of brave and excellent spirits; such as in my time was the Emperor Frederick the Second; who when he was indigent and in great necessity, was arrived to the Imperial Dignity, and brought under his obedience all Apulia, the Kingdom of Sicily, Jerusalem, Crocovia, Italy and the whole Empire (except Lombard) subduing all Enemies, Traitors and Rebels, and remained in that Illustratious flourishing condition; yet at last died miserably, being poisoned by his domestics, and all his family extirpated so that scarce any of them remained. Such an other was Ecilinus de Romano, who when he was but mean, was far exalted above all other Italians, for he ruled and, as it were, tyrannized over the Marquisate of Treves even to Almaine and Trent, and within four or five miles of Venice, and his Tyranny continued twenty-six years; but at last all these glories were overcast with calamity, for when it seemed impossible to suppress him, he fell into the hands of his enemies at a battle in the Country of Mediolanensi apud Cassianum, and died wretched, and all his posterity was destroyed, not one of them remaining. In the same manner there was in the Kingdom of Apulias of base descent, called Peter de Vinea: who when he was a scholar at Bononia was forces to beg for his living, and had not bread to eat, yet was made a notary, and after that Protonotary of the Court of the Emperor Frederick the Second; he became a Judge and climbed to such grandeur, that he was happy that could obtain the least of his favour, for whatever he did the Emperor would confirm; but himself would often set aside what had been established by the Emperor, who made him Lord of Apulin; whereby he grew so rich, that he had 10,000 pounds of Gold besides other Treasures almost inestimable; yet in the end he fell, and was reduced to such misery, that the Emperor ordered his eyes to be put out; enraged at which out of mere indignation he struck out his own against a wall, as it was then commonly reported. Another was at Pysa called Smerolus one of the drefs of the vulgar, who came to be, as it is said, Lord of that Province: nor durst any of the nobility for a while contend with him; yet at last he came to nothing. After whom one Gualduzius, a mean fellow, tapered up so high that he did as it were, sway the whole city and none would contradict him, till Galyver, a Judge, caused him to be chopped all to pieces. The same happened at Florylyciurn. One called Simon Mustaguere the son of obscure Parents, who mounted so high that all the people adored him: nor durst any oppose him, save only myself, who knew him thoroughly: and what mischief he could, he did at his pleasure for three years' space: but at last down he came being banished from the City which happened for the odiousness of his person and cowardice. Another being a Friar of the Preaching Order, by name John, by Nation Vicentinus, was admired as a Saint by all the Italians that acknowledged the Roman Church; but I ever thought him an Hypocrite; he grew so high that he was reported to have raised 18 from the Dead (though never one of them could be seem), and to cure all diseases, fright Devils, etc., yet could I not perceive anybody freed by him, though I made much enquiry into his miracles; however, the whole world seemed to run after him, and he thought himself happy that could get a thread of his Cap. Which they esteemed equal with the relics of the Saints; and in his preaching he would publicly boast, that he had Converse with Jesus Christ, the Virgin Mary, and Angels when he list. By which tricks, the Friars of his order at Sononia got more than 20,000 marks. And his power was so great that by his own will he released a Soldier as he was going to Execution for Murder; Nor durst the Magistrates deny him, not speak ill of him but myself, who knew all his wheadles and cozenages: for which the rabble, merely out of fear of him, reported me an Heretic. In which esteem and pomp he continued above a hear, but at last went out like the snuff of a candle, with a stink, his devices and hypocrisie being discovered, so that he became as generally: and everybody was ashamed to be seen in his company.

142. I42nd Consideration is, To observe in Nativities and general questions, the gifts and good advantages bestowed on men by the Planets: because those are applied more easily to them, and continue longer extended to their successors, according as they are well disposed in the Radicas of their Nativities; but they are seldom exceeding great, unless when applied by fortunate fixed Stars; because being of a more swift mutability they have ca closer affinity with them, especially if proceeding from the inferior Planets; for their conformity with men, their correlative subjects. Those of the Superiors last not so long with men but in building of houses they are much better than the other[6].

143. The 143rd Consideration, Is to understand the true method of judging, and by what ways thou mayest come to some result, that thou mayst examine and rightfully discuss the same, and

---

[6] NOTE BY LILLY : Of the Good given by Saturn and Other Planets, etc. ---Saturn Oriental and well disposed, that is strong and in Reception, gives great fortune in building, planting trees requiring a long growth, in manuring ground, erecting waterworks and the like. Jupiter gives good luck in Sciences such as the Law; and Dignities, being made a Bishop, a Judge, or the like. Mars in leading forth of Armies, etc. Sol in Lay Preferments, as Kingdoms, Governments, etc. But the Lower Planets bestow their gifts inherent to men and more durable: as Venus, in the attempts of women, their ornaments, courting them, etc. Mercury in trading, writing, etc. The Moon in navigation, planting vines, using drinks, selling wine, etc. All these, I say are excellently well bestowed by the Planets advantageously posited, and endure longer, that is to say, The prosperities given by the Moon may continue to the 7th year or generation, because she is the 7th planet reckoning downwards: and if they pass the 7th age or generation they cannot exceed the 8th as suppose from the 42nd year to the 45th year including those of Mercury may endure to the 6th age, being the 6th from Saturn, but will scare hold out of the 7th. Those of Venus to the 5th age, she being the 5th Planet from Saturn: but will not exceed the 6th. Those of the Sun to the 4th age. Those of Mars to the 3rd age. Those of Jupiter to the 2nd age. Those of Saturn only for one age, and cannot transcend; nay seldom reach the 3rd. And though I say they may continue so long, yet do I not say they shall not be finished before, for as Aristotle says, There are terms that cannot be passed over: yet he does not say but that they may be prevented and come short off so in these cases; and further, when I say that they cannot continue longer, I mean without vanishing wholly, or so depressed, that it will be no more like what was before, than green or russet to a perfect white unless by chance something from another cause happens anew; which seldom changes, nor can truly be said to be the same. But quite another thing from the first. Hence comes perhaps the common observation; that goods or possessions ill got, never abide to the 5th or 3rd age: many that use that proverb not knowing whence it comes to pass but only because they have heard others say so or seen it often happen thus. But from what we have here laid down, some reason may be given; for ill gotten goods count such as are got by way of usury, lies, deceit, theft, repine, and the like.

discover   the truth of what the stars shall show thee? And herein there are 14 points to be considered and heeded:

1. Whether the Querent proposes the question really and intentively or not? For if the Lord of the Ascendant and the Lord of the hour be in the same or the Signs wherein those Significators are   placed be of the same Triplicity or complection the Question is serious; but otherwise, if the Ascendant shall be the end of any Sign, the Question is not Radical.

2. Behold the Ascendant and his Lord, the Moon and the Planet from which she separates and   assign them for Significators of the Querent; the Seventh and the Planet with which the Moon is   joined, shall represent the person enquired after; but if it be necessary, descend to the persons, as the things are signified by the House, from the first to the twelfth.

3. Consider the nature of the thing enquired about, the House and Sign whereby it is signified.

4. The Aspects of the Planets both good and malevolent to the Significators of the things sought after.

5. In what place from its own House each of the Significators are: viz., Whether in his own or the second, third, or fourth, etc., or in the Combust way or the like places.

6. Whether they are found in Angles Cadent or Succeedent Houses.

7. Diligently see where the Querent's Assistants must come, viz., whether from a Father, a Son, a King a Kinsman, or a Friend, etc.

8. By the mirth of the Querent, as if the Lord of the Ascendant shall be in the fifth, or elsewhere   joined with its Lord; free from being afflicted by the Infortunes. Or by his sadness; as if his Significator happen in the 6th 7th 8th, or 12" ; unless the question be of things signified by those Houses; and as thou findest so judge.

9. By the Fortunes and Infortunes, according as thou findest them in places signified, the things about which the Querent is moved; and if the benevolents are more, 'tis good, if otherwise the contrary; if the testimonies are equal, then indifferent.

10. Whether the Lord of the Ascendant be in the House of the thing enquired after, or with its Lord.

11. In what House the Lord of the first is joined with the Significator of the things looked after; for by the Significator of the House, or his occasion, thou mayst judge the matter will be brought about.

12. If the Significators are not joined there, whether there be aby Translation of Light between them by any Planet, or receives their description, thou shalt judge the same thing.

13. By the natures of the Significators themselves, agreeing in their natures and significations with each other.

14. According to the receiver of the Significator's virtue or disposition shall be a Fortune or Infortune strong or weak, and does behold the Significator, or the Moon, or any with Aspect of love or enmity, so shalt thou pronounce judgment.

144. The 144th Consideration is, To observe in Questions, Nativities, or Elections, when the Significators shall not clearly show thee what thou wouldst know but the signifcation remains dubious, so that the mind is in suspense, take the place of the Lord of the Ascendant, and the place of the Lords of the Flouse of the Moon, and see the distance of degrees between them, beginning from Aries, of which make signs, and add the degree of the sign ascending: and project from the Ascendant as well by day as night, and where the number falls, the Lord of that House shall be Significator and from him take the Signification of the business enquired, for according to his disposition thou mayest judge.

145. The 145th Consideration is, That thou see in Diurnal Nativites, whether Cor Leonis be in the Ascendant, that is to say in the Oriental Line or above it one degree or below it three degrees; or whether it be in the tenth in like degrees, without the Conjunction or Aspect of any of the Fortunes; for this alone signifies that the Native shall be a person of great note and power, too much exalted, and attain too high preferment and honours, although descended from the meanest parents. And if any of the Fortunes behold that place also, his glory shall be the more increased: but if the Nativity be nocturnal, his fortune will be somewhat meaner, but not much; but if the Infortunes cast their aspects there it will still be more mean; but if the Fortunes behold it also they will augment the good promised a fourth part, and mitigate the evil as much; yet still what ever of all this happens, it signifies that the Native shall die an unhappy death; or at least that all his honours, greatness, and power, shalt at last suffer an eclipse, and set in a cloud.

146. The l46th consideration is, That thou take the place of the Lord of the Ascendant, and the place of the Lord of the 12th , and subtracting the lesser from the greater add to the remainder the degrees of the sign ascending and project from the Ascendant; and where the number falls the Lord of the sign shall be partner with the Lord of the Question, and shall be called the Principal Partner. Again, take the place of the Lord of the said sign, and place of the Lord of the Part of Fortune, and subtracting the lesser from the greater add the degrees of that sign shall be another Partner, and be called the Secondary Partner; which if it happen to be the same Planet, regard only that; but if different, then take both and subtract the lesser from the greater and add the degrees of the sign ascending, and the planet on whose House the number falls shall be the third Partner; and which of those three is the strongest shall be the chiefest sharer in the significations of the thing enquired after. If all the remainders, or two of them, shall happen on the House of one Planet; that shall be preferred. If the Question seem good, and those Partners are ill disposed, they will diminish of the good signified by the Question, and so on the contrary; but if the Question seem evil, and they are well disposed, they will allay and mitigate the evil signified by the Question, and so likewise on the contrary.

END OF THE CONSIDERATIONS OF GUIDO BONATUS.

www.ingramcontent.com/pod-product-compliance
Lightning Source LLC
Chambersburg PA
CBHW051014050726
47592CB00007B/2842